HAUNTED

HAUNTED

The Incredible True Story of a
Canadian Family's Experience Living
in a Haunted House

DORAH L. WILLIAMS

THE DUNDURN GROUP
TORONTO

Publisher: Anthony Hawke
Copy-editor: Elizabeth Phinney
Designer: Jennifer Scott
Printer: Transcontinental

National Library of Canada Cataloguing in Publication Data

Williams, Dorah L.
Haunted: the incredible true story of a Canadian family's
    experience living in a haunted house

ISBN 1-55002-378-0

1. Haunted houses — Canada. I. Title.

BF1472.C3W54 2002   133.1'2971   C2002-901063-2

    3   4 · 5   06   05

 Conseil des Arts **Canada Council**
du Canada   for the Arts

Canadä

ONTARIO ARTS COUNCIL
CONSEIL DES ARTS DE L'ONTARIO

We acknowledge the support of the **Canada Council for the Arts** and the **Ontario Arts Council** for our publishing program. We also acknowledge the financial support of the **Government of Canada** through the **Book Publishing Industry Development Program** and **The Association for the Export of Canadian Books**, and the **Government of Ontario** through the **Ontario Book Publishers Tax Credit program**, and the **Ontario Media Development Corporation**.

Care has been taken to trace the ownership of copyright material used in this book. The author and the publisher welcome any information enabling them to rectify any references or credit in subsequent editions.

J. Kirk Howard, President

Printed and bound in Canada.⊕
Printed on recycled paper.
www.dundurn.com

The events in this story are true.
The names of characters and some dates have been changed to protect the everyone's privacy.

Dundurn Press
3 Church Street, Suite 500
Toronto, Ontario, Canada
M5E 1M2

Gazelle Book Services Limited
White Cross Mills
Hightown, Lancaster, England
LA1 4X5

Dundurn Press
2250 Military Road
Tonawanda, NY
U.S.A. 14150

This book is dedicated to my children, for their open minds and open hearts; and to my husband, who now believes.

TABLE OF CONTENTS

1

THE OPEN HOUSE

I remember it was snowing heavily on that winter afternoon. We were all feeling restless, so Ted and I and our three young children went out for a drive in spite of the weather. The roads were slippery, and we remained on the town's ploughed streets rather than venturing onto the country roads. Eventually we found ourselves in the neighbourhood where we had lived when we first moved to town. I stared at the old Victorian houses and admired their distinctive character and charm but remembered how much work it had been to maintain one compared to the new house we had bought a couple of years ago.

An Open House real estate sign was propped up on the lawn of one of the houses. This surprised me as property in the area didn't go on the market very often. Ted pulled the car up to the sidewalk in front of the house and stopped. I looked over at him to see what he was doing.

"Why don't we go in?" he suggested.

"What? Why would we do that?" I asked, not really wanting to take three young children, bundled up in their snowsuits, on an idle tour of a house.

"I want to know what these houses are selling for now," Ted explained. Our old home had not been professionally appraised when we had sold it.

"But we sold our place two years ago. Prices could be a lot higher now," I asserted.

"It'll give us an idea anyway," he said. "I just want to know if the price we accepted for our house was fair."

Reluctantly, I unbuckled the little ones and headed towards the front porch. There were a surprising number of other cars stopping. The weather had turned so stormy that it was difficult to see across the street, but people kept arriving.

As we walked up the front stairs onto the porch, my reluctance turned to eagerness. What had at first felt like an unwanted chore began to seem like an adventure. While in the car, I would have preferred to wait with the children while Ted got a fact sheet on the house to settle his curiosity. But as I stepped onto the old wooden porch, my mood shifted.

The porch spanned the entire front of the house. While standing on its old wooden floor, I had a strong sense of the generations of people who had sat there discussing events that were now history. This feeling was so strong that I found it hard to resist going inside.

We entered the foyer. Its decoration did not reflect the age of the house but rather appeared to be right out of the psychedelic sixties. Blue and lime-green shag carpet covered the floor, and Ted and I smiled at each other in the mirrored tiles on the walls. We both knew what we thought of this style of décor.

The house did not seem to be very large. To the right of the foyer were pocket doors leading into the living room, or parlour, as it once would have been called, and straight ahead was a hallway that led into the kitchen. The staircase leading up to the second floor, with its beautiful oak newel post, was located on the left.

We walked through the pocket doors into a large living room. It was somewhat dark and gloomy, and faced north. The roof of the expansive porch in front of its only window prevented much of the daylight from entering the room, and a large weeping willow tree that draped over most of the front yard further blocked the light. Directly opposite the pocket doors was a fireplace. Its bricks appeared to have been replaced, although the original hearth still remained.

Off the living room was the dining room. This room faced south and was therefore a bit brighter. A doorway there led into the kitchen, which boasted its original cupboards along the west wall. They must have been quite beautiful in their day, serving as built-in china cabinets. Now, however, a dull blue paint covered many other layers, and they were falling apart. Unfortunately, they were past restoring and would need to be replaced. On the north side were two matching interior doors with elaborate glass doorknobs. One door opened into a large pantry, and the other led downstairs to the basement.

The back door to the house was on the kitchen's south side. Outside was a rickety old porch with stairs leading down into the small backyard. At the edge of the lot stood a dilapidated shed that had probably served as a stable or small barn decades ago. It now appeared to be on the verge of collapsing.

After our tour of the first floor, Ted went in search of the real estate agent to obtain an information sheet while the children and I went upstairs to look around. We had a lot of stairs in our new house and none of the children had ever fallen, but this particular staircase made me feel ill at ease. I warned all of them to be careful and held tightly onto two-year-old Rosa's hand. Once at the top, my nervousness was gone, and I wondered why I had been so bothered in the first place.

The second floor was very compact. It contained four bedrooms and a bathroom, all leading off a hallway. Three of the bedrooms and the bathroom appeared to have been recently decorated, and they, more than any other area in the house, seemed to reflect the Victorian era. The fourth bedroom, though, did not appear to have been used in a very long time.

As we wandered from room to room, I could feel my enthusiasm increasing, but I could not justify it. I felt surrounded by a warmth that was strangely comforting. The atmosphere in the house was really positive, and I sensed we would be so happy living there.

I smiled as the children each chose which bedroom they would have for their own, even though we already had a house and were there only for a moment. Matt, who was almost five, was delighted with "his" room because it had a door that led to another flight of stairs up to the attic. That was the one bedroom that had not been redecorated with the others, and it was musty with disuse. It seemed to have been closed off for years and opened only now for the Open House. The door leading up to the attic appeared to have once been boarded up as there were nail holes in the trim, but now it stood open.

I again held Rosa's hand and cautioned the children to be careful as we ascended the narrow flight of stairs up to the attic. It was half finished, but rough. Although the space was not at all attractive, it was at least useable. It was lit only by two small north windows, and its walls were covered in navy blue paint. Properly refinished, it would have made a wonderful office, den or perhaps even a play room for the children.

Meanwhile, Ted was downstairs taking note of the old windows that needed to be replaced and the plumbing and wiring that had not been updated since the house's construction at the turn of the century. When the children and I finally tracked him down, he was in the basement examining the floor joists to see if they were sound. The asking price listed on the fact sheet was quite a bit lower than what we had sold our neighbouring house for two years before. Although it was not decorated as nicely as ours had been, it was a larger discrepancy than we had expected. It was quite a low asking price for a place in such a desirable neighbourhood.

I looked at my husband for a moment, and was about to say something, but stopped myself and headed up the stairs to the first floor. I put on my boots and the children followed my lead, but I did not yet feel ready to go. I told Ted I wanted to take one more look around, and he nodded in agreement and went with me up to the second floor.

"What's on your mind?" he asked.

I smiled at him, thinking he would laugh at me for even considering buying this house.

"I don't know why, but I just love this house. And it's such a good deal," I began.

"It's a bit small for us. Besides, what would we do with another house?" Ted said.

"We could always build an addition," I answered his first objection, and the real estate agent, overhearing our conversation, quickly agreed that that would be no problem whatsoever.

13

"I get such a good feeling from this house," I whispered to my husband as I admired the original claw-footed tub in the nearby bathroom, "but those stairs make me kind of nervous."

"Why? What's wrong with the stairs?" Ted asked.

"I don't know. I'm just afraid someone is going to fall there," I tried to explain, but I did not really understand the feeling myself.

"These stairs aren't as steep as the ones in our house," Ted reasoned. "And look at that oak railing. They look pretty safe to me."

He put his arm around me, and we walked back downstairs.

"We'll do some thinking about it," Ted told the hopeful real estate agent as I took one last look around before we left.

The children talked about the house all the way home. The girls were thrilled with the bedrooms they had chosen, and Matt marvelled over the stairway that led from "his" bedroom up to the attic. Except for Ted's initial reservations, it seemed that the house had had the same effect on all of us.

After much discussion and debate, we decided that we really did want to move to the old house, although we could not rationalize its great attraction. It would need a lot of redecorating. Every room would have to be redone eventually to suit our taste, and we knew we would have to cope with the expense of building an additional family room for extra living space. The lot on which the house stood was only a quarter of the size of our own property. There was a mortgage on our current home, and Ted had only been in his position with a new firm a few months. The timing could not have been much worse for making such a move.

We contacted the real estate agent and asked for another showing of the house. If we went through it again, we thought, we might realize that purchasing it was a ridiculous idea. One afternoon the following week, while seven-year-old Kammie was in school, Ted, Rosa, Matt and I went to see the property. It seemed quite a bit larger now that it was empty of all the people who had been milling about during the Open House. I noticed things that I had overlooked, such as the beautiful antique light fixtures and the original iron radiators with their ornate Victorian design. I realized it would not be impossible to restore the house back to its turn-of-the-century splendour. It would just take a lot of hard work. Rosa, meanwhile, had raced to the bedroom she had claimed and excitedly cried, "My room! My room!"

During the second showing, Ted saw that the house was very solidly built, and he noted the extra beams that had been placed in the ceiling of the basement to give additional support to the main floor. Even more so than during my first visit, that house just felt like "home." We had had to move a few times since we got married due to Ted's career and had owned two other Victorian houses in the past. We had been fond of them, but I had never had the same sort of feeling in either of them that I had there. I could appreciate its history despite its décor and felt a very odd, strong sense of belonging.

We met the owner, Mr. Ryan. He was in his mid-seventies and in poor health. I assumed that was the reason he was selling it. He seemed delighted that a "nice young family" such as ours was considering buying his home. He had lived in the house for over twenty years, and it was important, he told us, that the new owners felt right to him. Although we had once lived only a block away, we had only shared a friendly smile and a polite "hello" with Mr. Ryan on our occasional walks past his house. He did not seem to remember us, but the children had grown and we now had Rosa, so our family would have looked a lot different to him.

Before we could purchase the old house, it was necessary to sell our new home. We were not usually impulsive, yet we began advertising our new home so our family could move out of it and into a very old house that needed repairs, remodelling, and redecorating.

Ted, especially, had been proud of the new house. But he wanted to move into that old home as much as the children and I did.

It would later seem incredible to us that we even considered such a move at that point in our lives. Everyone we knew thought we had lost our minds and did not hesitate to tell us so. Why would we want to move into an old "money pit"? But we had made up our minds, and it was a great relief when we found a young couple who wanted to purchase our house. The transaction did not net us all the money we had put into it, but it was close enough. With that, the financial obstacles we had thought might be insurmountable were actually easily overcome, and Mr. Ryan happily accepted our offer.

On a beautiful spring morning three months after we first saw it, we moved into the house. When we arrived, Mr. Ryan was still there, although all his possessions were gone. I found him standing in the dining room, staring out into the yard.

"Will you look at that," Mr. Ryan said quietly as he gazed out the window.

"Is anything wrong?" I asked him.

"Oh, no dear," he assured me. "It's just that my magnolia tree is finally blooming."

"Oh," I replied, not fully understanding the significance of that.

"We received that tree as a gift from my niece when we first moved into this house. Every year I hoped it would bloom like that, but it never did. In fact, it has hardly even grown at all since it was planted. I just came in here to have one more look around, and what do you know? It's in full bloom! That's a nice housewarming gift for you, isn't it?" The old man smiled rather sadly, then prepared to leave his home for the last time.

I looked out the dining room window and saw the small tree enveloped in gorgeous white blossoms.

THE OPEN HOUSE

"That must be a good omen," I thought happily and began to unpack the first of our many boxes.

When Kammie came in, she too was greeted by a lucky sign. She found coins lying in the middle of the floors and on window sills and countertops, and she went around to all of the rooms picking them up. When the other two children realized what Kammie was doing, they too joined in on the treasure hunt. I was surprised at the number of coins they collected as I knew Mr. Ryan had hired a maid service to give the house a thorough cleaning before we arrived. I had not noticed a single coin anywhere, yet the children soon found them.

2

STEPS THROUGH TIME

During our first few months in the house, we were busy with non-stop renovations. We fixed the kitchen walls, floors, ceiling and cupboards. We finished the attic, put up new shutters, replaced all the windows, and added two new ones in an attempt to gain some much needed sunlight to brighten the dark interior.

I painted and wallpapered, choosing colours and patterns I imagined might have adorned the walls when the house was originally constructed. First, though, layer upon layer of ancient wall paper had to be removed. Nine different patterns had covered the foyer walls in the past ninety years. Even the ceilings had been wallpapered several times, and it was a tiring and painstaking job to remove it before fresh paint could be applied.

Returning the house to its original beauty became almost an obsession, one I had not experienced with the two other older homes Ted and I had owned. And I had only wanted to achieve a warm and "homey" feel in our last new home, which had been easily done using bright colours and contemporary furniture. That old house, in contrast, seemed to have a personality of its own, and I felt a strong desire to uncover and if necessary re-create its Edwardian era charm.

We still had not built the new family room or replaced the dilapidated shed in the backyard. Those projects had to wait until we could afford them, for we had encountered enough expensive problems. When the shag carpet had been pulled up from the floors prior to moving in our furniture, we discovered that someone had poured cement beneath the rug to affix it to the original oak flooring. Because of this damage, all the floors had to be professionally refinished. When that was completed, though they gleamed as they must have when first installed.

By the end of the first year, even before the redecorating was completed, it looked like an entirely different house. It had been transformed into a beautiful and charming Victorian home. It would take time before everything was decorated the way we wanted it, but I was prepared to work away, one room at a time, for as long as necessary. I left the girls' bedrooms and our master bedroom. Although the wallpaper in those rooms was not of our choosing, we could live with the patterns until all the other areas were finished.

Matt's bedroom, though, could not be put off. Its walls were a hideous grey-brown from years of dust, and cobwebs had needed to be swept from its corners when we had first moved in. It looked as if it had not been used for generations, which I thought very odd. Mr. Ryan had several children and grandchildren who had visited him regularly and surely he could have made use of the space. I could understand sealing off the attic, if only to save on heating costs, but why had that room been closed off as well?

I felt uncomfortable working in the room, but I thought it was simply because of its drab appearance. The atmosphere would be much nicer once it had been painted and decorated. My little boy wanted a hockey theme in the room, as that was his favourite sport, and I found the perfect border to match the paint and paper. The other rooms in the house were decorated in Victorian and Edwardian style, but the children had been allowed to choose whatever colour and pattern they wanted for their own bedrooms. Kammie wanted her room to look like a forest, and Rosa wanted teddy-bear wallpaper.

Matt's room looked completely different when I was finished. He was happy with its fresh look, but he had been drawn to that room even before it had been cleaned and redecorated.

It may have been because we were so busy those first few months, or perhaps we just assumed what we were hearing was the natural creaks and groans of an old house, but it was some time before Ted and I began to notice the sound of footsteps running down the stairs between the first and second floor. On many occasions we would sit in the living room after putting the children to bed and hear someone descend the stairs into the foyer, continue down the hall, and enter the kitchen. We always assumed it was either Kammie, Matt, or Rosa. I would order whomever it was to stop running on the stairs in case they fell. And Ted would sometimes call, "Come on out. We know you're up," in case the child did not realize we knew they were out of bed and hiding in the kitchen. A glance, however, always revealed an empty stairway, and none of them ever appeared where we were seated.

HAUNTED

Even the children remarked on hearing the sound of footsteps, but it did not bother them. It gradually became so commonplace that after a while we just accepted the peculiar noise and paid it little attention. Another oddity we all came to accept was the wonderful aroma of bread or cookies baking that mysteriously and frequently wafted through the house. It seemed to emanate from the kitchen even though I had nothing cooking in the oven. Even stronger was the distinctive smell of a wood-burning cook stove. Ted and Kammie noticed that phenomenon the most and would often comment on it.

Shortly after we began to hear the footsteps and smell those aromas, I tried to learn as much as I could about the previous owners of the house. I visited the local history section at the library and the downtown land registry office. Through that research, and conversations with elderly neighbours who had lived on the street for many years, I learned that the property had had seventeen different occupants, including us. Old telephone books proved to be a valuable source of information as they listed not only the address and name but also the owner's occupation and spouse's name. The town's newspaper, saved on microfilm, also provided a lot of detail, and I read as many back issues as I could.

One family had lived in the house for forty years, and another had resided in it for nine. Mr. Ryan had sold it to us after living there for two decades. Apart from those three families, all the other residents seemed to have come and gone rather quickly, and there were many years when the house had sat altogether vacant.

I knew the house had been built in 1903, as our home and several of our neighbours' houses had all been constructed in the same year. That fact was verified by many elderly residents and by the old town records. I could not establish who the land's original owner had been through the telephone directories at the library, as that form of communication had not yet existed at the time the property was sold. At the land registry office, however, I learned that on March 29, 1865, the property upon which the house now stood, which had once been Crown land, had been sold to a Mr. F. Lincoln. At that point, the town's small population had been growing steadily and there were a few industries, including a carriage factory, tannery, and mill.

Mr. Lincoln had kept the property until April 9, 1879, when he sold it to James Raye. On March 10, 1880, Mr. Raye, in turn, sold it to Walter Smit. By that time the property was only half an acre in size and the price paid was $450. The local economy was good, and based on newspaper advertisements from that period, eggs sold for only ten cents a dozen, a pound of tea, for less than forty cents, and flour, was six dollars a barrel.

By the time of Walter Smit's death, on June 23, 1903, the property had been divided into three small lots, each boasting a brand new house. Mr. Smit left the property to his son Walter Jr., who then sold the house we would one day own only a few days later to Robert Hudson for the sum of $2,150. Mr. Hudson kept the house for only four months, selling it on October 29, 1903, to Ivan Wards Jr. for a price that was illegible in the old record book.

Mr. Wards apparently left the house less than six months later. The records seemed to indicate that it had been repossessed by the financial institution that held the mortgage because the payments could not be honoured. Or Mr. Wards simply chose to walk away from his monetary obligation for some other reason and allowed the bank to repossess the house only half a year after purchasing it. His father must have decided to live there next. The house sat empty and the bank was unable to resell it to any other purchaser until July 29, 1905. On that date, for the bargain price of $1,300, someone named Ivan Wards Sr. became the next owner of the house.

Mr. Wards did not live there for any longer than his son did, however. After six months, he also moved out and sold the house in early January of 1906 to Mr. Evan Albertson for $2,600. At that time, automobiles were still quite a rarity and the nearest mechanic was over a hundred miles away. The central location of the house must have made it very desirable as it was only a short walk away from all the town's amenities. Those would have included the first movie houses, which, for a five-cent admission price, played silent films that were changed three times a week.

Four years later, on April 16, 1910, Fredrick Barker bought the property for $3,150. Mr. Barker and his wife lived there only until October 11, 1911, at which time they moved just two doors away, leaving the house vacant.

In April of 1912 the whole world was stunned by the tragic loss of the *Titanic*. But locally 1912 was a prosperous year, and the real estate market was booming. Still the house remained vacant. It was not until 1917 that William Neen became its next resident. His occupation was listed as baker and then as soldier. Apparently he was renting the house from the Barkers because the property remained in their name. When I saw that he had been a baker, I immediately thought of the aromas that teased us in the house, and the wood-burning cook stoves that would have been used for baking in 1917.

Mr. Neen was not mentioned after the end of the World War I, and I wondered if he had ever come home again. Whatever might have been his fate, there was no record of a wife. The house remained vacant again until August 30, 1919, when Mrs. Barker, now a widow, finally sold it to a Mr. and Mrs. Ford for $3,050. That was less than she and her late husband had paid for it nine years before.

Of all the former owners of the house, the Barkers' actions intrigued me most. Why would they leave the house eighteen months after its purchase only to move two doors away into an identical house on the same street? The appearance, layout, and dimensions of the two houses were exactly alike. I could have understood their moving if the house two doors away had been larger, or had had a different floor plan, or if they had moved to a different location. But the only visible difference between our property and the one two doors away to which the Barkers relocated was that the lot was two feet wider.

What seemed even stranger to me was that the house had sat vacant for such a long time, given the neighbourhood's preferred location. That would have been the case even more so early in the century, with its close proximity to the downtown core. Other than the Barkers' eighteen-month residency and the one-year period in which it had been rented out to Mr. Keen, no one had lived in the house at all in the eight years the Barkers owned it. In a time when real estate sales were brisk and buyers were eagerly seeking houses, why could the Barkers not sell the house when they had no intention of using it themselves? And why did only one person rent it during that period when, according to an old newspaper article, housing was in such high demand? Finally, why, when Mrs. Barker was able to sell it, had she taken a loss on what they had paid for it several years before?

I went back to the library to do more research and noticed some strange patterns I had not noticed before. Not only had the Barkers abandoned the house after eighteen months to move two doors away, but the first two owners had also stayed for just a few months before moving within the same neighbourhood. Robert Hudson had lived there for only four months when he moved down the street, eight houses away. The next owner, Ivan Edwards Jr., stayed for six months before leaving, and he too bought another house right around the corner. Obviously those former residents liked the neighbourhood as they chose to remain in it. They must have liked the style of the home because

25

HAUNTED

their next ones looked identical. Why then had they not simply remained in the house?

Another unusual coincidence I detected was that, with only two exceptions, one of them being our family, every new owner of the house seemed to come from out of town. It seemed as if only strangers to the area, those unfamiliar with local history, were willing to purchase and then live on that property, but in most cases, not for very long. We had been in town for six years when we purchased the house, but we had not been very familiar with its local history either. Yet my search through the newspaper archives did not uncover any report of an unusual or tragic event ever taking place at that location.

From August 30, 1919, until May 22, 1927, the Fords lived in the house. Until then that was the longest period that anyone had resided there. The Ford family had been similar to ours, with two little daughters and a son.

When Mr. Ford sold the home on May 22, 1927, to G. J. Niles, he received $4,500 for the property. That was a very good price for the time. Mr. Niles and his wife, Jenny, lived in the house the longest time of any owner. They too had a family that consisted of two daughters and a son. The wealthy Niles family, who wanted to have a house in town so it would be easier for their children to get to school, also owned a country property that served as their weekend residence. The house would not change hands again until 1968.

Our next door neighbour, Donelle Porter, had lived in her home for most of her life. She liked to remind people that she was older than the grass in the neighbourhood, because most of the land had not yet been sodded when her family moved into their new home. Her parents had purchased the property when it had been first built, and she remembered all of her previous neighbours very well.

26

When she was young, Donelle and her siblings had been very good friends with the children who had lived in our house. She remembered Mrs. Niles very fondly and often spoke of "Aunt Jenny," as everyone in the neighbourhood had affectionately called her. They had been kind and thoughtful people who were always ready to help out their neighbours, especially during the difficult years of the Great Depression. Donelle's mother would very thoughtfully be presented with a crate of oranges and grapefruits from the Niles each Christmas, and the significance of that generosity was still evident in our elderly neighbour's reminiscence.

In July of 1968, Luis and Martha Borgin bought the house from the Niles and lived there until August 1970. Luis had an accident and was forced to move to a nursing home shortly before they sold the house to its next owners, Martin and Pamela Riley, in August 1970. However, the library's records indicated that, although they bought the house, the Rileys never actually lived there. The house was listed as "vacant" until it was sold again three years later to the next owner.

Mr. and Mrs. Ryan purchased the house in 1973. They lived there with their children for quite a while until Mrs. Ryan passed away in the hospital after a lengthy illness. Then, with his children grown and on their own, Mr. Ryan found the upkeep of the house too difficult with his frail health. So, after more than twenty years of ownership, Mr. Ryan sold the house to our family.

Although my research did make me curious about the former residents of our house, I did not find anything in the written records, such as a death or a fire, to explain the occurrences we were later to witness. It did, however, seem peculiar to me that the property had changed ownership so frequently. Since it was first purchased, seventeen different residents had moved in and out of the property over the years, with only a few staying a substantial length of time.

Our elderly neighbour Donelle seemed to know all about the current and former occupants of every house along our street, and she helped me to fill in the blanks in my research that the library's records could not. She entertained us with stories of the "olden days," and the children loved to hear her talk of her own childhood. A lot of the area had been farmland, so our neighbourhood contained some of the oldest buildings in that part of the town.

Donelle told us about the people who had lived in our home before we did, but nothing out of the ordinary was ever mentioned. It seemed as if it had always housed happy, normal, growing families, very much like our own. Donelle went into great detail about the children who once lived there and what had become of them as they married, began careers and moved away. Although some of them had unfortunately died early in their lives, as young adults, no parent had ever lost a child while living under that roof. As far as we knew, and we certainly had not been told otherwise, there should have been nothing unusual about the house itself.

When events began to unfold, we did not know why. I went back to the local history section of the library many times looking for answers but could find nothing there that offered an explanation.

I felt it would be inappropriate to question Mr. Ryan or Donelle about specific occurrences. It was obvious that Mr. Ryan had left his home reluctantly. When we bought the house, he had told us, very sincerely, that his family had shared many happy years there and he hoped that our young family would do the same. I did not want Donelle to think I was crazy, so I asked only general questions about the past. And, I did not want to reveal that I was trying to determine if someone from a former time was haunting our home. After all, perhaps the incidences were not related to the actual house but were linked somehow specifically to the piece of land, or even just to our own family.

I realized as time went on that a haunting was a private matter. It was not something easily discussed with other people, even a close neighbour. If we felt we could not tell others about the happenings within our home, then perhaps former residents had felt the same restriction. If they too experienced strange occurrences, they may have felt the only option they had was to move away. And that certainly had been done, time after time.

3

WATCHING FROM THE WINDOW

During the days, while Matt and Kammie were at school and Ted was at work, Rosa and I kept ourselves busy in our new home. Our cocker spaniel, Piper, loved to follow us around but refused to go up the stairs to the second floor. She had not hesitated to do so in our previous house, but now, if we went upstairs, she would sit on the foyer floor and cry until we came back down. If one of us carried her up, she would dash into the master bedroom, jump on the bed, and shake like a leaf until she was brought downstairs again. She would occasionally remain in either Kammie or Rosa's bedroom for a short period of time, but would whine and run for the door whenever Matt tried to bring her into his room.

We fully expected Piper to resume her old habit of sleeping every night at the foot of one of the children's beds and thought she only needed time to get used to the new surroundings. She continued, however, to avoid our second floor. As with the footsteps on the stairs and the mysterious odours, we gradually came to accept her strange behaviour.

Life went on fairly smoothly, despite those oddities. The children seemed to love our new home, and Rosa often played in the backyard with Piper while her brother and sister were in school.

One afternoon, Rosa came running into the house from the yard, yelling, "A pretty girl is up in my bedroom!"

"Is she?" I smiled at her when she reached me, but I was a little surprised. It wasn't like Rosa to make up stories. She was so emphatic and excited, however, that I could not help but chuckle.

"I saw her! She was standing at the window up in my bedroom and she waved to me!" Rosa persisted.

"What did she look like?" I asked, playing along with what I thought was a new game.

"She had on a pretty dress and a bow in her hair," she said.

I was beginning to feel uncomfortable with Rosa's seriousness.

"Sweetie, no one is here but you and me. And I wasn't upstairs," I explained to her.

Rosa insisted that we go up to her room to see if the girl was still there. I thought it would help to convince her that she had just imagined seeing someone waving to her from her window, so upstairs we went, hand in hand. The room was empty, of course, but Rosa remained unconvinced.

She walked over to the window and looked down to where she had been playing in the yard, blowing bubbles with liquid soap and a bubble wand.

"That's where I was when I saw her," Rosa said and pointed. "And she was right here at the window, waving to me." She was growing frustrated with my disbelief.

"But you and I are the only ones in the house," I said again.

Rosa nodded her head in agreement, but I could see she was confused. She knew what she had seen, but she also understood that we were the only people at home and that no one else was in the bedroom.

"But I saw her. Where did she go?" Rosa asked.

I shrugged my shoulders in response and hoped that was the end of it. But Rosa walked over to her closet door and peeked inside, then looked under her bed, still searching for the girl who had been at the window. Thankfully, after a few moments she gave up and went back outside with Piper.

Rosa mentioned having seen the same girl on a number of occasions over the next few months, but she was much more casual about it.

"I saw her watching me today," she would say.

"Who?" I would ask, thinking she was referring to one of our neighbours.

"The girl in my bedroom," would be her calm reply.

Her older sister and brother laughed at her insistence that she had seen the girl. They questioned Rosa about her story, trying to get her to trip over her facts, thereby proving she was only making it up.

"Did you see that girl again, Rosa?" they would sometimes ask when they arrived home from school.

She would usually admit that she had not seen her that day but occasionally she would relay her sightings to them, never wavering in the details she gave. Kammie and Matt thought it was a fun game to play, and Rosa enjoyed thinking they really believed what she claimed. After several weeks Rosa stopped talking about the girl, and the matter was all but forgotten.

Shortly after Rosa ceased to mention the girl in the window, our family prepared to go away for a few days. Before we departed, I made sure all the lights were off and the doors securely locked and inadvertently left my purse on the oak cabinet in the foyer. Upon that cabinet was a large, Victorian-style oil lamp framed by two small family portraits. It was positioned directly opposite the front door. I went back in and picked up my purse, giving the hallway a glance as I headed out the front door, and made sure the foyer light was turned off before I locked up.

When we returned, I unlocked the front door while Ted unloaded the suitcases from the car in the driveway. I immediately noticed the oil lamp as I walked into the house. The glass chimney that sat on the lamp's base was now upside down and wobbling on its tip. I stared at it for a moment, unable to believe what I was seeing. I knew it had been properly positioned before we left. Kammie came up behind me and immediately noticed it too.

"Why did you do that to the oil lamp?" she asked me.

"I didn't touch it," I said, trying to sound calmer than I felt.

"I don't think you should leave it like that. It looks like it's going to fall," she replied before heading up to her bedroom.

I picked up the delicate glass chimney and attached it properly to the base. When Ted came in with the suitcases, I told him how I had found it.

"One of the kids must have done it," he said, dismissing it with a logical but impossible explanation.

"When?" I asked. "It wasn't like that when we left, and no one else has been in the house."

He just shrugged his shoulders, and we said nothing more about it.

4

THE FLOATING WOMAN

By the end of the first year the only major home improvement project that remained was the addition of an extra room onto the back of the house.

We hired an architect to design some plans for the new room and spent a lot of time deciding how and when it would be built. Construction would begin in early spring and we decided, as well, to replace the old shed with a new one. We were very eager to get those projects underway, and Ted and I stayed up late one night discussing the plans, the cost, and other details. I found it difficult to get to sleep after our conversation and tossed and turned for what seemed like hours. Ted, as usual, fell into a deep sleep as soon as his head hit the pillow. I lay in bed, facing the bedroom door that led out into the hallway, listening to the sound of his snoring.

The hallway was lit by the collective glow of the night-lights from each of the children's bedrooms. That light spilled into our room, making it easy to see, even in the middle of the night. After laying on my right side with my eyes closed, trying to get to sleep, I sat up slightly in order to turn over and face the other way. I opened my eyes, and froze. A dark figure was standing at the door, blocking the glow from the hallway. As my eyes began to focus, the figure before me grew clearer, and I realized it was a woman.

I was terrified by the sudden appearance of that figure but I could not look away from it. I wanted to turn to Ted and shake him from his sleep, yet could not make myself move. The woman appeared to be extremely tall, and I wondered if she were floating several inches above the floor. That thought scared me even more, and though I desperately wanted to awaken Ted, I could not move a muscle.

Her figure was very dark against the light, but I clearly could distinguish her clothing and hair. She was wearing a cape of some kind and was draped from head to toe. The idea came to me that she was dressed like a nurse from many years ago. I could not understand why, as her clothing was quite different from a present-day nurse's uniform, yet the thought had been very clear. The headpiece hung like a veil behind her, and the long cloak covered her dress. Her hair was curled in tight, small ringlets and was clearly visible in front of the head piece. I could see it in astonishing detail; it was as though I could discern each strand of hair. Yet, though I could so easily make out her hair and clothing, I could not see her face. Instead I stared into a blank dark space, void of any features. Even in my shocked and frightened state, that seemed particularly bizarre.

After several very long seconds, I was finally able to move and leaned over to where my husband was laying. I buried my face in his back and shook him until he awoke. As he had been sleeping deeply, it took him a few moments to become aware of how upset I was. When I looked towards the doorway where the figure had been floating, I saw it was gone. The light from the hallway now streamed in unobstructed. I jumped out of bed and hurried in to the children's bedrooms to see if they were all right, and found them all sound asleep.

When I returned to our bed, Ted tried to assure me that I must have been dreaming. There was clearly no one about, and it would have been impossible for anyone to enter the house without our dog barking protectively. The stairs were so creaky that you would have heard someone approaching long before you saw them. I knew all of that to be true, yet the woman had been there. And then she was gone.

"Are you sure you weren't dreaming?" Ted asked.

"I haven't even been to sleep yet," I said.

"There must be some explanation," he mumbled through a yawn.

"I don't want to sleep on this side of the bed anymore," I said irrationally. I could not explain why I thought that that particular side of the bed was now to be feared, but I would never sleep there again. That night Ted and I changed places, and I preferred to lay facing the window rather than the doorway.

As I lay beside Ted, knowing that falling asleep would be next to impossible, I remembered Rosa's frustration when she had told me about the girl waving to her from the window. She had known I did not believe her, and she had been confused by how the girl had appeared and then vanished. I now regretted my doubt and empathized with her feelings.

The next day, I was frightened to be alone in the house. I sensed I was being watched and found myself constantly looking around to see if anyone else was there. I was so disturbed that I seriously thought we should consider moving. I recalled the speedy departure of most of the house's former residents, and I could not help but wonder if they too had seen something similarly frightening. The sound of running footsteps on the stairs, formerly deemed harmless, now seemed to have an ominous quality.

When everyone was home at the end of the day, I mentioned that I thought it might be a good idea to sell the house and move. The children, unaware of my fears, were very surprised because I had worked so hard on decorating the house and it was finally looking beautiful. They reminded me that the new addition was all planned and building would begin in the very near future and told me they loved living in the house and did not want to leave. I did not want them to be terrified by thinking that they lived in a "haunted house," so could not tell them what I had seen.

Ted understood how upset I was. He told me we would do whatever I thought was best, but I could tell that he did not want to move either. I knew it was hard for him to accept what I claimed to have seen. He knew I was not lying but insisted there had to be some logical explanation for it; he certainly was not about to believe we shared our home with a ghost.

I felt as if there was really no one I could talk to about the sighting, and I found myself trying to rationalize it. Maybe it had been only a dream. Yet I knew I had been wide awake at the time. Perhaps I had only imagined it. But the vision had been too detailed and had stayed before me too long for that. I tried to find any explanation to convince myself that it had not really happened. I did not want to believe we shared our home with a ghost, either.

A few nights later, I was again lying in bed unable to sleep, with my eyes tightly closed. Suddenly I became strongly aware that I was about to be touched. I could sense someone leaning over me as if about to pat my hand in comfort. I opened my eyes fearfully as I was certain someone was standing right beside me. When I looked, no one was there. I sighed with relief, but the feeling of being watched persisted. When I awoke the next day, however, I felt very peaceful and no longer felt an urgent need to move from the house. I thought that whatever I had seen the other night was now gone, and the presence I had felt leaning over me seemed to have left as well.

The children were relieved when I told them that I did not think we should sell the house after all, and life carried on. We continued to plan for the new addition to the house, and, one night, invited our neighbour Donelle over for dinner. The conversation around the table soon turned to the time when she had been a young girl and friends with the children who had once lived at our address. I asked Donelle about the Ford family, who had lived in the house from 1919 until 1927, even though the clothing of the woman I had seen seemed to be from an era quite a bit earlier than that.

"Was Mrs. Ford a nurse, by any chance?" I asked her casually.

"She may well have been before she got married, but I can't recall for certain," Donelle mused. "They were a very 'medical' family, with lots of doctors, nurses, pharmacists and the like, I do remember that."

Everyone ate in silence for a while and then Donelle again spoke.

"The thing I remember the most about Mrs. Ford, though, was that she was an unusually tall woman," she said. "She was the tallest woman I have ever seen in my life!"

I almost choked on my food before I glanced across the table at Ted. The apparition I had seen in our bedroom doorway had been strikingly tall. Could it have been Mrs. Ford? Without seeing a picture of her, I could not be sure. But since the apparition had had no face, even a photograph could not have answered that question. I wondered if I would ever solve the mystery of who she was and why she had been there.

5

BURIED TREASURES

Our household was soon preparing for the construction of the family room and shed in the backyard. We were all looking forward to having extra living space, and the new outbuilding would definitely improve the appearance of the property. When we had first tallied the cost of all that work, we had mulled over the idea of closing in the front porch instead of building a room at the back of the house. The porch was quite large and would have made a nice sun room for a lot less money than the addition we were considering.

Ted had taken measurements and priced the material necessary to transform the porch into a large glassed-in sitting area. He had crouched down on the front walkway beside the stairs and shone a flashlight beam through the lattice to get a good view of the space underneath.

"What did you find under there?" I asked him when he came back into the house.

"Just some crushed rubble that must have been the last set of stairs. I guess they just demolished them and shoved them under the porch," he replied.

"Were there any old toys or anything like that?" Kammie asked her father.

"No. Nothing but big pieces of broken cement and lots of dirt," he answered.

We finally decided to go with the original plan of adding an extra room at the back of the house and to leave the porch as it was.

The shed was built first, and it seemed to go up quickly. Our contractor was ahead of schedule, and we were pleased with how well everything was coming along. Construction of the new room began, and one of the work crew spent the first few days digging deep holes in the ground for the footings. Despite the difficulty of the task, he eventually managed to dig down several feet into the hard, rocky earth. The children enjoyed watching the men working and kept an eye on their progress. Kammie especially seemed to marvel at how deeply the holes were dug and shyly stood at the corner of the yard to see what the shovels of dirt revealed.

The next afternoon I heard Kammie call out "Mommy!" from the backyard.

I rushed out and found my daughter standing by one of the holes, clasping something in her small hands.

"What?" I asked.

"Look what Stuart gave me," Kammie said, smiling at the builder with gratitude.

"What is it?" I asked again.

"It's a really old glass jar," Kammie said. "Can we clean it?"

I nodded. We walked over to the garden hose spigot, and I sprayed off most of the grime. Then we took it into the kitchen and held the muddy jar under hot running water. Eventually the final layers of dirt dissolved, and we saw it was a small white jar. It was made of thick glass and measured about two inches high by two inches wide. It appeared to have once contained cream or a cosmetic. It was fairly ornate, with delicately engraved columns, in contrast to the plain cream jars of today.

"Where did Stuart get this?" I asked my daughter.

"He found it when he was digging the hole deeper. He said I could have it!"

"I wonder how old that is," I murmured to myself as Kammie continued to polish the glass.

"Isn't it pretty?" she asked, admiring it with great delight. "Where should I put it?"

I wondered how the jar had come to be buried so deep in our backyard and who had originally owned it. Perhaps another little girl had been given that fancy jar by her mother or grandmother once the product had been used and had treasured it, many years before.

"Why don't you put it in your room?" I suggested to Kammie as I started to prepare dinner.

When Ted came home that evening Kammie could not wait to show him what had been discovered in the footing hole. He looked at it for a minute, smiled at her, and told her she was very lucky to have found such a nice jar.

"Well, Stuart found it," Kammie corrected him. "But he said it's mine now, and I can keep it." She carefully carried the antique glassware back up to her bedroom.

When I tucked her in that night before going to bed, I smiled at the sight of her happily snuggled up to the little jar lying on the pillow beside her. She must have fallen asleep while admiring it. I placed it on her dresser and kissed her good-night.

After school the next day Kammie raced home to see if Stuart had found any other treasures for her from deep within the ground. She was not disappointed. Waiting for her by the pile of dug-up dirt was an antique ink-well. Stuart had found it at the very bottom of the same footing hole. It was slightly smaller in size than the glass jar, and was made from clay glazed a brownish-yellow. It was in very good condition. That artifact, which appeared to be quite old, excited Kammie even more than the glass jar had, and she spent a long time cleaning it. For a quill she used an old feather she had found, that I had cleaned for her, and stuck it into the top of her newest find. The glass jar and clay ink-well were then placed side by side on her window sill, and everyone who visited that spring was invited to view her antique items.

After those finds, Kammie began digging in the flower beds and other parts of the yard, searching for other things of value. She concentrated her digging in an old garden plot, now located beside the wall of the new addition. When I asked her about that activity, she explained that she had a feeling there was some kind of treasure buried in the yard and she wanted to find it.

Kammie's digging unearthed a large rock, close to where Stuart had found the other items, which appeared to have been splashed with gold paint. She told me about her discovery several times during the day, but I was working away at wallpapering and did not go out to see what she had found. It was not until after dinner that evening that Kammie asked me to take a look at the rock to see if I thought it really was gold she had discovered.

Ted and I looked at each other and smiled at our daughter's naive enthusiasm, but I followed her into the backyard to examine her find. She could barely lift the heavy rock and struggled to pick it up to be inspected. As I bent down to take it from her small hands, I caught my breath. The rock was almost completely covered with quartz and was streaked throughout with a shiny gold colour. Kammie had spent a lot of time spraying off the dirt with the garden hose, and the rock now sparkled in the late day sun. I called Ted to come out and look at it, not quite knowing what it was that Kammie had found. Maybe it really was gold.

Ted's reaction was similar to mine. He casually walked out of the house, thinking I was just humouring our daughter with feigned interest. When Kammie passed the rock to him, the smile faded from his face and his jaw dropped a bit. He stared at it and then at us, speechlessly.

"Where did you find this?" he finally asked Kammie.

"Over there," she said, pointing to the overgrown spot that had once been a garden.

"When?" he said.

"After Stuart left today. I was digging in the old garden looking for something," Kammie explained.

"What do you think?" I asked Ted. "Could it really be gold?"

"It sure looks like it, doesn't it?" he said

We decided to contact a friend of Ted's who worked as a geologist. She would know what it was that Kammie had found. When Ted telephoned her, she asked him to bring the sample over to her house so that she could have a look at it. While he and Kammie drove over to see her, I stayed at home with Rosa and Matt.

It turned out to be only pyrite, better known as "Fool's Gold," but Ted learned some interesting history about the town, and our property in particular, that evening. His friend told him that well over a hundred years ago, before there was any kind of town in our area, there had been a gold-rush of sorts. A river had once run right through our neighbourhood, and it was in that body of water that people thought they were discovering gold. It caused quite a commotion for a short period of time until everyone finally realized it was not gold at all but pyrite.

Perhaps, then, some former gold prospector, or someone who knew him, had buried that large sample of pyrite on our land. Or maybe our backyard had once been the site of the short-lived but very real "rush" that ended in much disappointment. If the prospecting site had not been located right on our property, it had been very close by, and the rock could be a souvenir of those earlier days. It might have once belonged to someone like Kammie, who regarded it as valuable because of its beauty and not its economic worth.

I had thought she would be disappointed that her discovered rock did not contain real gold, but Kammie was still thrilled with it. She proudly took the exquisite sample of pyrite to school the next morning for Show and Tell.

"See?" she said to me. "I knew there was something buried in the backyard."

"How did you know that?" I asked her. "Did you learn in school that fool's gold had once been discovered here?"

"No, we didn't learn anything about that. I'm not sure why, but I just had a feeling about it. Something made me want to look there for a special buried treasure. It was like I knew it was out there somewhere," Kammie said. "And I finally found it."

The last item Stuart found for Kammie was an antique glass button that had been buried close to the other items in the yard. I took it from him to clean before it joined the other objects Kammie now owned. He also found several bones in another location. When he mentioned that to us, quietly, so the children could not overhear, I felt my stomach tighten.

"What kind of bones?" I asked, dreading the answer, for I remembered something Donelle had told us.

BURIED TREASURE

After Kammie had shown her the items found in our yard, Donelle had reciprocated by showing us an arrowhead that she had found and kept from her own property and explained that our neighbourhood had once served as a Native encampment. In fact, one of the oldest homes in town, built in the mid-1800s, was near our house, and you could still see the original heavy wooden shutters inside the windows that had been installed to protect its inhabitants from any possible attack. Its close proximity to the encampment and the fact that the house had been built on Native land had obviously caused its owner to nervously expect a retaliation that never came.

Given Stuart's discovery, I was afraid that our house might have been built on an ancient burial ground. Ted knew exactly what I was thinking and asked Stuart to show him what he had found. When Ted saw the bones, it seemed evident to him and to all the other men at the site that they were actually the remains of a large animal, probably a horse. I was greatly relieved that they were not human bones, of course, but was still unhappy that an animal carcass had been buried right by our back door. Ted assured me that the partial skull and two leg bones were probably from the time long ago when our neighbourhood had been farmland.

I never did see the bones. They were put into a truck along with other debris and then removed from the site by the contractor. And, as I had hoped, no more were ever found.

During the week that the contractors were digging, the frequency and intensity of strange occurrences increased inside the house. I did not immediately connect the two, but it soon became obvious that the construction of the addition had triggered that increase. We had been living in the house for two years, and had only experienced a few odd events in that time that could not be logically explained. Those events had been sporadic, and although unnerving, were easily forgotten in the long intervals between their occurrence. During those periods, we were a happy family living in a lovely home and our life seemed perfectly normal. But, with the construction of the addition, our household stopped seeming "normal" altogether.

6

AWAKE IN THE NIGHT

A short time after the construction began, we were all awakened late one night by the shrill sound of a smoke detector. Ted and I quickly leaped out of bed to establish which of our many alarms was signalling the warning. The screech was coming from the alarm in Matt's room. Though we could detect no trace of smoke, the detector relentlessly sounded, and Ted had to dismantle it and remove the battery before it fell silent. As it was a fairly new detector, and we had recently replaced all the batteries in the alarms on the weekend we switched to daylight-saving time, we could not figure out why it had malfunctioned. It took a while for us all to get back to sleep after that incident.

The next day I purchased and installed a new battery for the alarm in Matt's room, in case the old one had been faulty. That night, however, I was once again disturbed from a sound sleep when Matt suddenly began calling for me. I went into his room and found him sitting up in his bed, looking very frightened. He was so upset that I had to hold him on my lap and calm him before he could tell me what was wrong.

"Did you have a bad dream?" I asked him, assuming a nightmare had frightened him. He shook his head and clung to me tighter. "Try to tell me what's wrong," I said softly.

"I woke up," he said quietly.

"Yes, you woke up," I said. "What frightened you?"

"I woke up," he began again. "And there was a lady sitting on my bed looking at me!"

I stared at him for a moment. Obviously something had terrified Matt, yet I wanted to believe he had only imagined that vision. I did not want to consider that the ghostly image I had seen was still present in our house.

"What did she look like?" I asked him.

"I think she was a church lady," he said.

"What do you mean?" I asked, puzzled by that description.

"You know, those ladies with the long hats, like in the movie? She looked like that," Matt tried to explain.

I realized he was referring to the film *The Sound of Music*, which we had recently watched on television.

"Do you mean a nun?" I asked.

He nodded his head.

As we had watched the movie only a few days earlier, I thought it might be possible that Matt's memory of seeing the nuns in the film had triggered a similar dream.

"Were you dreaming about a nun and then woke up and thought you saw her?" I asked.

"No," my little boy said, firmly shaking his head. "I felt some-one sit down on my bed and it woke me up. When I turned around to see who it was, there was a church lady sitting where you are."

I knew he was telling the truth. I also realized that the woman I had seen had been dressed very much like a nun. I had assumed she was a nurse, but the veil and the cloak could have been a nun's habit or might at least be mistaken for one.

I wanted Matt to know that I believed him, but I also hoped to make him feel safe.

"Did she look friendly?" I asked.

"She wasn't smiling," he whispered fearfully.

Unlike my sighting of the woman, Matt had obviously been able to see her face. If I had been terrified by the sight of her figure before me in the doorway, how frightened my little boy must have been, waking up to see a strange woman on his bed, staring down at him, while the rest of the family was sound asleep in other rooms.

I brought Matt into our room and let him sleep at the foot of our bed in his sleeping bag. He fell back to sleep almost immediately, but I was unable to rest at all.

The next morning, after Matt and Kammie had left for school and Rosa was happily watching cartoons, I went into Matt's room and sat on the edge of his bed. In the bright light of day it looked like a typical little boy's bedroom, with wallpaper featuring hockey players, toys and books scattered about, and artwork covering the dresser and bookcase. Yet I could not forget the fright I had seen on Matt's young face the night before. Now that one of my children had been affected, I was much more angry than afraid of whatever it was that was present in our home. I decided to try to talk to whomever or whatever had sat down on his bed.

"I won't have you scaring my children," I said, speaking just loud enough to make myself heard but not to disturb Rosa in the living room below. "Maybe this used to be your home, but we live here now. I don't want you making your presence known to us any more," I said firmly.

The house seemed calm and quiet after I had spoken to this presence, and we all slept through the next few nights undisturbed. Then Matt called out to me once more in the night, and I again went in to comfort him. When I entered his room, he mutely pointed to the door near his bed that led up to the attic. Always firmly closed at night, it now stood wide open.

"The door opened up all by itself," he told me nervously.

I closed the door, made sure it was properly latched, and then sat down on his bed.

"Who opened the door?" he asked.

"I think it just wasn't closed properly and swung open on its own. Things like that can happen in an old house," I said, trying to calm his fear, despite my certainty that I had closed it tightly when I had tucked him into bed.

"Can Piper sleep with me tonight?" he asked. I nodded my assent and went down the stairs to the living room to get the dog. I hoped that, on that occasion, she would stay with Matt and comfort him. Piper snuggled happily into my arms when I picked her up, but as we approached the stairway to the second floor, she started to tremble. When I brought her into Matt's room and put her on the bed with him, she immediately jumped down and dashed into the master bedroom. I found her hiding under the covers of our bed, beside Ted.

I tried again to have Piper stay with Matt but she simply refused to do so. I finally closed the door of his bedroom so that she would not be able to leave. Just as I was about to lay back down in bed, Piper began howling desperately, frantic to get out of Matt's room. That sound woke up the other children. Even Ted awoke, after sleeping through all the other commotion.

"What's wrong with Piper?" Kammie called out sleepily.

"We can't let her do this all night," Ted grumbled, looking at the clock that told him it was only a little past 3 a.m.

I went back to Matt's room. The minute I opened the door, the dog burst out, shaking with fear.

"Matt, I think Piper only likes to sleep downstairs," I said, not wanting him to know that it was only in his bedroom that the dog refused to stay. "Would you like to camp out in Mommy and Daddy's room tonight instead?"

He nodded eagerly. After I tucked him into his sleeping bag atop our bedroom carpet, I took a relieved Piper back down to the living room.

The next morning Ted and I had a long talk about what had been happening in our house. We decided that, if we were not going to sell the property, then we would at least do some rearranging and let Matt have another room. We could move the two little girls into one bedroom. Their rooms appeared to be undisturbed, except for Rosa's past insistence that a girl occasionally waved to her from her bedroom window. We thought Matt would feel more secure in a different room, and we could use his current bedroom as a den or a day-time play room for the children. I recalled how that particular bedroom had not been used prior to our purchasing the house, and I thought I now understood why that had been.

When Matt came down for breakfast we shared our idea with him. We fully expected him to happily agree to the new arrangement.

"I don't want to leave my room," he said, to our amazement.

"Matt, remember how scared you were last night? Don't you think it would be better if we just put you in another room, and then you wouldn't have to worry about the attic door or anything else like that any more?" his father asked him.

"I like my room the best. I want to stay there," Matt pleaded.

53

We were puzzled by his reluctance.

"Honey, you can't sleep in Daddy and Mommy's room every night, and it seems like sometimes you're scared in your bedroom. Wouldn't you feel better sleeping in another one from now on? We can decorate it any way you like," I coaxed.

He shook his head again. He told us he never wanted to move and insisted he would not be afraid in his bedroom any more.

"Okay," Ted sighed. "You can stay there for now. But we don't want to be awakened every night. If you keep getting scared in there, we'll have to make other sleeping arrangements."

Matt seemed immensely relieved and ate his breakfast contentedly while Piper sat by his side.

That night I was awakened yet again by our son's cries. I rushed into Matt's room and found him trembling under the covers. The temperature in his bedroom was freezing. I walked over to the radiator and touched its icy side and realized I would need to call a repair man. The heat from the furnace was obviously not reaching his room, although the rest of the house was quite warm.

"What is it?" I asked him softly.

"Someone's walking down the attic stairs," he whispered. We sat together and listened but heard nothing. "It's stopped now. But I heard footsteps walking down the stairs and stopping at the door," he told me.

I opened the door that led to the attic and turned on the light. Matt felt calmer upon seeing that no one was there. As I had done the previous night, I closed the attic door and ensured it was properly latched. Then I pulled his heavy wooden toy box in front of it. I showed Matt that it would be impossible for the door to be opened then as his toy box was blocking the way, and that seemed to remove all of his fear.

"Are you okay now?" I asked, reluctant to leave him alone. He nodded sleepily and turned over. "Do you want to camp out in our room tonight?" I suggested.

"No, it's okay now," he said bravely, as I put an extra quilt over him to keep him warm.

I went back to our room but found it difficult to rest. I kept straining my ears, listening for footsteps. I did not doubt what Matt had told me. We had all heard running footsteps on the main staircase, and I would be frightened, as Matt had been, if I heard them approaching my bedroom door late at night.

During the days, the kids were happy, the dog was content, and our life seemed to be ideal. At night, however, the house seemed to take on an eerie quality, and I was finding it more and more difficult to sleep. I had never suffered from insomnia before, but I lay awake for hours, wanting to rest, but listening for sounds instead.

Matt must have been tired as well because his sleep was often interrupted. Besides the recurrence of the footsteps on the stairway coming down from the attic, he also insisted that he had heard them in the hallway outside his room and on the stairs leading up from the foyer.

One night, after he had called out and I went in to check on him, he told me he had seen something round floating near the ceiling with a long, thin tail hanging down all the way to the floor. He was unable to describe it properly. He said he had not seen anything like it before, and it had been a different shape from that of a person, but that was all he could tell me about it. He did not seem as much frightened by it as mystified.

The next day I gave him a pencil and paper and asked if he could draw me a picture of what he had seen in his room. He immediately started to draw a strange object that resembled the funnel cloud of a tornado, but just what it was that he had seen was no clearer to me.

On the exceptional nights when I had fallen asleep and Matt remained undisturbed, a smoke detector would inevitably go off somewhere in the house, jarring everyone awake. The smoke alarms were becoming a very serious problem for us. We had a total of nine detectors installed throughout the three-story house. Within a six-month period, the alarms sounded a total of nineteen times, always around 3:00 a.m. and for no apparent reason. Regardless of where they were located, or whether they were battery operated or wired into the electrical system of the house, all of them went off at one time or another. It bothered us that none of them ever shrilled during the day when everyone was up and wide awake. Nor did they ever go off while I was lying sleepless in bed late at night. The detectors only screeched when every person in the family was in a sound sleep.

After detecting the chill in Matt's room, which I had noticed only after construction had begun on the addition, I called a furnace repair man to fix the problem. We had replaced the furnace shortly after we had moved in. It heated the rest of the house very efficiently, and the persistent chill in Matt's room was a mystery to the repair man I called time after time. He could detect no mechanical failure, although he checked both the furnace and the radiator several times to ensure there was no blockage. Each time he was there he managed to get the radiator heated, but within hours of his departure, it would grow cold. I stacked blankets and quilts on Matt at night to keep him warm.

By the time the addition was completed and all the furniture was in place, both Matt and Kammie were on summer vacation from school. We celebrated Matt's birthday by holding a party for him in the new room. Then, the following morning, we packed up the car and headed north to our family's cottage on the coast for a much needed holiday. It was so peaceful for us there. Everyone slept soundly, with no interruptions at all.

On the day we returned home, I walked through the house and the new room and out the back door. I started down the stairs to the backyard but stopped on the first step and stared straight ahead at the tree growing next to the wooden fence between our property and Donelle's.

The previous year we had noticed a small walnut tree starting to grow in the grass near the property division, apparently after a squirrel had buried a nut there and forgot to retrieve it. It had been only a very small sapling when we first noticed it, and several times Ted had accidentally run over it with the lawn mower, cutting off its top. Because Donelle had told us that walnut trees emitted a poison to surrounding vegetation, Ted would occasionally mention that he was planning to get rid of it. Yet the tree had not seemed to pose a threat to our garden or the grass that grew in abundance around it.

By the time the new room was completed, the sapling had grown slightly higher than the six-foot fence. Its top had been severed where Ted had cut it with the lawn mower, and only a few scraggly limbs had branched out from its thin stem. I had videotaped the addition's progression, and the small tree was clearly visible on the tape.

Now, only weeks after those images had been captured, I stood looking at the same tree in disbelief. It towered over the whole corner of the property. It had become so large that it covered not only Donelle's kitchen window on the first floor but her bedroom window on the second. She would no longer be able to watch the children and Piper playing in our yard, which was one of her favorite pastimes.

When Donelle saw Ted unpacking the car upon our return from the cottage, she called over to him, and told him she wanted that tree pruned. He did not understand her request until I called everyone into the backyard. We all stared at the walnut tree in shocked silence. I watched Ted as he slowly shook his head in disbelief. How could the tree have grown so much in such a short period of time? It was beyond our comprehension.

7

SOS

Soon after our summer holiday, my sleep was disturbed one night by Kammie calling me to come to her room.

"Mommy!" she cried. "Come and see what my bonker lamp is doing!"

The children's grandfather had recently given them new bedroom lamps similar to one they loved to play with at his house when they visited. They were not switched on like an ordinary lamp but were turned on and off with the touch of a hand. Because Rosa made a "bonk" sound whenever she touched her lamp to turn up the light or turn it off, the children now referred to their gifts as "bonker" lamps. The first touch turned the light on, and the next two caused the light to grow increasingly bright. On the fourth touch, the light would turn off.

I gasped as I sleepily entered my daughter's room and saw the lamp on the small dresser beside her bed. All three of the children's new lamps were left on low at bed time as night-lights. Instead of glowing with its usual low light, the lamp in Kammie's room was quickly blinking from low to medium to high illumination, then turning off. At a slower speed it again began to go from low to medium to high, in a steady pattern.

Kammie thought it was hilarious and howled with laughter. "It's doing it all by itself!" she roared.

I called for Ted to come and see. He walked into the bedroom and stared at the blinking light.

"There must be a power surge," he suggested.

"But the other two lights aren't blinking," I replied, trying to sound calm.

The three of us continued to watch as an unseen hand seemed to tap the lamp over and over again, turning it on, then turning it brighter and brighter still, and then off, only to begin again. It went on for quite a long time. Ted suggested that it might be caused by lightning, but the sky was perfectly clear. The children had had their new lamps for a few months, and none of them had behaved like that, including Kammie's.

"Fast, fast, fast, slow, slow, slow, fast, fast, fast..." Kammie kept saying, as she called out the light pattern we were witnessing. The only way to stop the light was to finally unplug it.

The next day we plugged the lamp back in, and it functioned normally. It did so for the most part, but occasionally it would turn itself on and then grow brighter and brighter and then off, over and over again.

Kammie never tired of this entertainment and would call us into her room each time it happened. "Fast, fast, fast, slow, slow, slow, fast, fast, fast..." she would call out along with the pattern of the light. We tried switching lamps. When placed in any other bedroom, Kammie's lamp never malfunctioned, nor did any other lamp placed in her room. But when we switched them back at her request, within a day or two her lamp began to "bonk" out the now familiar pattern on its own.

Although Kammie found the lamp amusing, there was an occurrence in her room during that same period that she did not like. Throughout her childhood she had been collecting glass globe ornaments that appeared to contain falling "snow" after they were given a slight shaking. Several of the globes were musical. If the tab beneath them was cranked, they would play a melody.

The large collection of globes was kept on two very high shelves in her bedroom. Neither Kammie nor Matt could reach the ornaments. Even Ted could not reach them without standing on a chair. Yet, on several occasions that summer, two particular globes would simultaneously begin to play their melody. Certainly they had never done so before, although Kammie had owned those globes for years. One had a nativity scene and played "Away in a Manger." The other contained a grouping of angels. Its song was "Lara's Theme." Those melodies would play only in the middle of the night, waking Kammie. Then her calls to me would wake the rest of us.

The tinny sound of the musical globes in the stillness of the night was incredibly eerie. The music only played for a few moments if the globes were cranked by hand, but on those occasions when they turned on by themselves, it was almost impossible to get them to stop. I could understand why Kammie found that so unsettling; I too was frightened by it. At her request, I removed the entire collection out of her room and placed the globes in an unused cupboard downstairs. Once moved from her room, they remained silent.

We then displayed her china dolls on the shelves. These too eventually had be to moved into storage. Kammie, with Matt as her witness, insisted that the head and limbs of the beautiful doll dressed in pink had moved as if someone were playing with it. I hoped they had only imagined that. Still, the fear in Kammie's eyes was quite real, and I did remove all the dolls, because she was afraid to have them in her room.

Shortly before the end of the summer we took a weekend trip out of town. The night we returned, everyone settled into bed for a sound sleep. Ted and I were covered with only a light sheet, as it was a fairly warm night. I awoke after someone poked my right big toe through the bed covering. I lay still for a moment, groggy with sleep, before I felt it again. Ted was lying with his back towards me, so I knew it had not been him. I was not startled; I just assumed it was one of the children wanting me for something.

When I again felt my toe being poked, I sat up slightly to see which child was trying to get my attention. As I could see no one there, I sat up fully, and as I did so, I felt one last child-like poke against my toe. When I got up to check on the children, they were all fast asleep in their rooms. I lay awake for a long time after I returned to bed. Shortly after I had managed to doze off, the smoke detector in the hallway right outside our room began screeching, and I rested no more that night.

I was reluctant to mention the strange incidents to anyone outside our family because I knew how difficult they were to believe. Ted lived in the same house yet even he insisted that there had to be a logical explanation for everything that had happened. Other than during the incidents with her globes and doll, Kammie did not really seem to be bothered. I doubted if Rosa gave it very much thought at all, aside from those occasions when she had seen a girl waving to her from her bedroom window. And although I thought Matt had the most reason to fear being in the house, he seemed to love living there the most, at least during the day.

I was feeling so exhausted from lack of sleep though, that I could barely think straight. I did not know what to do or where I could turn for help. We had worked so hard to restore the house, and it looked beautiful, but I did not think I could stand to stay in it much longer. Yet the children became upset if I even suggested moving.

Finally, during a long-distance telephone conversation with a friend, I confessed everything that had been happening in our home. I had known Sylvia Norton for most of my life, and I felt comfortable confiding in her. She listened quietly while I listed all the events that had taken place. By the time I had finished telling her about the latest incident from the night before, when someone or something had poked my toe and then set off the smoke detector, I was close to tears.

The desperation in my voice convinced my friend that I was serious about those "ghostly" events. She responded by asking the obvious question of why we did not simply leave. I explained to her how attached to the house the children seemed to be and how Ted did not want to sell it either. His work kept him so busy that moving our household was the last thing he wanted to think about. Sylvia then asked if we had crosses hanging anywhere in the house. We did not. She suggested that I purchase some religious items and place them in the rooms that seemed to have the most unusual activity.

After our telephone conversation, I went shopping. I bought a cross to put on the wall in Matt's bedroom. Although our family did not attend church on a regular weekly basis, the children had been taught about God and Jesus from an early age and bedtime prayers were a part of their bedtime routine. I knew that Matt would understand the significance of the cross, and I hoped having it there would make him feel safer in his room at night.

When he came into the kitchen after school that day, Matt gave me a big hug.

"Hi," I said. "That's a nice greeting."

"Thank you, Mom," he said.

"For what?" I asked, not realizing he had already been to his room.

"Thank you for putting that cross up in my bedroom. I really like it," he answered.

It surprised me that he had noticed it so quickly and that he was so grateful for it. I explained to him why I had put it there.

"Are you going to put one in Kammie's and Rosa's room too?" he asked.

When I showed him the framed prints I had purchased for the girls' rooms of a guardian angel helping two lost children across a bridge, Matt seemed relieved.

"Can you put them up now, Mommy?" he asked anxiously, and I agreed to do so.

The children seemed so happy with those items that we soon added similar artwork. Above Rosa's bed, we hung a painting of a blonde, curly haired guardian angel wearing a long pink dress. She liked it so much she insisted upon kissing it goodnight before going to sleep each evening. In Matt's room, we put up a picture of a little shepherd boy watching baby Jesus sleeping in the manger. Above Kammie's bed, we hung a picture of another blonde, curly haired guardian angel.

Following Sylvia's suggestion, I soon had the children's rooms adorned with religious items that I hoped would create a more peaceful atmosphere. I did not expect that all the strange occurrences would stop because of a few items, but I hoped they would be helpful in some way. But, to my relief, everything seemed to settle down completely. No one saw anyone or anything that frightened them, no smoke detector blared its alarm in the middle of the night, and the footsteps on the stairs seemed to disappear altogether. Our house became an ordinary home and everyone, including me, began sleeping through the nights undisturbed.

I called Sylvia back to tell her of this development and to thank her for her suggestion.

"I've been thinking about everything you told me, and I was going to give you a call tonight," she said. "Does that lamp still blink out that pattern?"

"No, we've put it away and replaced it with a new one that operates with a switch," I told her.

"You said the pattern it flashed out was fast, fast, fast, slow, slow, slow, fast, fast, fast, right?" she asked.

I affirmed the pattern of the lamp's activity for her, but wondered, given all the bizarre events I had told her about, why she was so interested in it.

"I looked up Morse code on the Internet..." she began. Upon hearing these words, I immediately felt uneasy. It had not even occurred to me that the pattern of the blinking light could be a coded message of some kind.

"What does the pattern mean?" I interrupted.

"Ready for this? Fast, fast, fast would be 'S.' Slow, slow, slow would be 'O.' And, then fast, fast, fast again for another 'S.' SOS is the message," she told me.

"God," I said nervously. "How are we supposed to help?"

That conversation soon receded from my mind, however, when everything remained calm within the house. I only hoped it would stay that way.

With all that had taken place over the summer, I had forgotten to send out the photographs taken at Matt's birthday party. When I received the developed photos back in the mail, I sat down to glance through them. I could not help but smile at the cute, happy faces of my own children and the other party guests enjoying the funny antics of Klinky the Klown, whom we had hired to entertain everyone. One particular photograph, though, made me pause. I asked Ted to have a look at it.

The picture showed Klinky the Klown doing a magic trick with Matt assisting him. Several children could be seen seated on the sofa and floor around those two, all laughing at the funny act. But unlike the other photographs, taken from the same angle, only seconds before and after, in this one there appeared to be two bright bubbles of light hovering over the seated children. One was approximately the size of an adult's head. The other was smaller in size, much like the head of a child. Ted and I examined the photograph carefully, trying to determine what could have caused the orbs of light to appear. As no explanation was evident, we eventually shuffled the picture back in with the rest. I wondered, though, about a camera's ability to capture on film what the human eye could not see.

With that in mind, I went out and purchased a new roll of film. The next time I found myself alone in the house, I walked around the rooms with my camera in hand, taking pictures.

"If you're here, could I take your picture?" I called out as I entered Matt's room, but felt foolish doing so. It had not occured to me to ask permission in any other room. There had not been any unusual activity for some time, and I had no reason to think a presence might be nearby. Still, I thought it might be a good opportunity to see if anything out of the ordinary could be captured on the last shot left on the roll of film.

I took the film to a local one-hour developing lab and waited anxiously to see the photographs. All the pictures were ordinary shots of empty rooms except the one I had taken in Matt's bedroom. In the centre of the photograph, on the north wall, several feet above his bed, I could see a semi-transparent face staring straight at the camera.

When I arrived home, I hurried to locate a magnifying glass. I then lit the photograph with a bright light and examined it again through the lens of the glass. The face was now much more obvious. I studied the eyes, eyebrows, and nose, trying to determine if the face was male or female. Although it was hard to determine, I thought it was a woman. When I remembered the "church lady" Matt had seen in his room, I also thought that the face appeared to be framed by a headdress.

When Ted arrived home from work and we had a moment alone, I showed him the picture and asked him if he noticed anything unusual about it. He immediately pointed to the face.

"What the hell is that?" he asked, taking the photo over to the better light near the window.

"Does it look like a face to you?" I asked him.

He nodded and handed the picture back to me in silence. The idea of that image being so close to our little boy's bed unnerved us both.

We continued to study the photograph closely for a few more minutes, trying to determine if the image of a face might have been caused by a flaw in the negative or a problem during the film's processing. Then I scanned the photograph into our computer to see if I could enlarge the image, but the impression was so faint that it was not possible to see it clearly at all. As we had no way to enhance the image, we could not really be positive of what the camera had captured.

Even though Ted and I had convinced ourselves that the image in the photograph was too faint to be identifiable, at dinner that evening we again casually raised the subject of Matt moving to a different bedroom. As in the past, he pleaded with us to let him remain in his current room. Because nothing had recently frightened Matt and he obviously wanted to stay there, Ted and I later privately agreed not to bring that up with him again.

Autumn passed into a very cold and snowy winter. Everything inside the house remained quiet and seemingly ordinary; even the heat in Matt's room had been restored. It had been so long since anyone had been awakened in the night that it was easy to forget how difficult those experiences had been. I remarked to Ted that it seemed incredible that something so simple as putting up a cross and pictures of angels in the children's rooms had solved all the "haunting" activity we had endured. He said he was happy if the pictures made us all feel better, but I could tell he did not take the effectiveness of those items as seriously as the rest of us. I did not bother to ask him why he thought the activities had stopped as suddenly as they had begun; I was so relieved that everything was peaceful again that I just wanted to forget they had ever happened.

Later that month, we visited a local museum with the children. We were wandering through the building looking at the artifacts when we rounded a corner and almost walked right into a mannequin. It was part of an early medical exhibit, on loan from the museum of a nearby town for a short period of time. There were many photographs of various local nursing staffs from the late 1800s onwards lining the walls, dressed in the traditional white dress and cap. The mannequin, however, was dressed like the figure of the woman I had seen in our bedroom doorway, and judging from the startled look on Matt's face, like the woman he had seen sitting on his bed. He studied the display intently and then looked over at me. I smiled at him and nodded to indicate that I knew he recognized what he saw, which brought some relief to his face.

The flowing cape and headdress resembled a nun's habit more than a recent nursing uniform, but the information plaque beside the display explained that nurses had worn that uniform many years before the more contemporary dress shown in the photographs. The only difference between the petite mannequin before me and my memory of the apparition I had seen was in their size. The spirit, although similarly dressed, had been very much larger, especially in height.

8

OUT OF THIN AIR

While leafing through a Victorian interior design magazine one day, I happened upon an advertisement for a studio that specialized in reproduction vintage portraits. They transferred the faces from a favourite picture to an actual antique portrait and, by using computer technology, transformed it into a turn-of-the-century photograph. A large antique wedding portrait of Ted and me would serve as the finishing touch in our master bedroom, so I chose a picture from when we were first married and selected one of their vintage photos for the transfer.

After several weeks, I received the beautiful portrait in the mail. From the style of clothing and hair, it appeared to have been taken well over a hundred years ago, and I had bought an antique-style frame in which to hang it.

The day it arrived, I had to take Rosa to a doctor's appointment and had only a few minutes to spare before we had to leave the house. As the frame was waiting in our bedroom, I decided to place the picture in it to see how it would look. Once I had admired it for a moment, I was eager to see it hanging on the wall. I thought it would only take a minute to do that, so while Rosa waited at the front door, I rushed to get the hammer, and the picture hanger and nail that I had bought with the frame. After determining the best spot to hang the portrait, I started to strike the small nail through the hanger and into the wall. In my haste, I dropped the hanger, and it, along with the nail, fell with a clatter onto the hard wooden floor in our bedroom.

I did not want us to be late for the appointment, so I impatiently got down on my hands and knees to retrieve the dropped items as quickly as possible. The picture hanger was on the floor directly below where I had been hammering, but the small nail was nowhere to be seen. In my frustration I thought to myself, "I need that nail," as I searched all over the floor for it. It should have been near the hanger but it had completely disappeared.

Suddenly I heard the clink of something fairly heavy hitting the wooden floor directly beneath me. At first I could not understand what had caused the sound, because I knew nothing had dropped from my body. When I looked down at the floor, I saw a large and rusty nail. I stared at it in disbelief. Where on earth had it come from? It certainly had not been in any of my pockets. And I kept our home clean enough to have noticed a large nail like that lying in the middle of our bedroom floor.

I picked up the nail and tried to understand what had happened. The smaller one that I needed to hang the picture had fallen to the floor and completely vanished. While trying to locate it, I had concentrated on a "nail" and one had materialized right beneath me. I thought that was the most bizarre event that had happened in the house, because it had produced a tangible item I could hold in my hand. Obviously it was not just a product of my imagination, and yet there was no plausible explanation for its appearance.

The nail was much bigger than the one that I had lost; I thought I could not possibly use it to hang the portrait. Still, someone or something had known I was looking for a nail and had made one appear. I put it away in Ted's tool box until I could show it to him. Even he would not be able to explain the incident away with logic, and it was concrete proof that something extraordinary had happened even though he had not been there to witness it for himself.

When Rosa and I arrived home after her doctor's appointment, Ted was already there. I quickly got the nail for him to examine.

"What are you doing with this?" he said.

"How old do you think it is?" I asked, before telling him my story.

"I'm not sure, but it's pretty rusted. They used nails about this size for the footings, I think, when they were building the addition. Maybe it came from there. Where did you find it?" he asked.

I proceeded to tell Ted every detail of what had happened that morning. When I described the sound I had heard beneath me and how I had looked down to find the nail lying on the floor, Ted looked at me strangely and then started to laugh. That was not the reaction I had expected.

"What's so funny?" I demanded.

"Well, if this is something the 'ghosts' did, they must really be trying to drive you crazy," he said, laughing again.

"What do you mean? They were trying to help me," I insisted. "They knew I needed a nail and they gave me one."

"If the picture hook nail really did disappear and this was given to you to replace it, don't you think that's funny? You don't help someone by taking away the nail they need and replacing it with a huge one like this that you can't even use for hanging a picture," Ted said.

I had not thought of it that way at all. I had believed that somehow someone had known I was in need of a nail and had made one materialize to help me. But why had the small nail disappeared in the first place? Maybe Ted was right. Maybe it had not been intended to help me, especially if it was the same kind of nail that had been used in the building of the new room that had caused us so much disturbance.

Ted maintained that it was a joke on me that such a huge nail had appeared when I was trying to hang our portrait. Several months later, though, we heard a loud crash and hurried into our room to find that the large portrait had fallen onto the floor. The nail I had used to hang the heavy frame was not strong enough and had dislodged from the wall. Why the fragile glass covering the portrait did not break upon impact was a mystery to us, but when I picked up the frame, I realized that it never would have fallen if I had used a larger nail. Perhaps the one that had materialized beneath me that day had been meant to help me after all.

Although nothing unusual had occurred in our home for many months, I somehow sensed that the appearance of that large, rusty nail was the beginning of the end of the quiet period we had enjoyed. Thinking back, I realized that all the nightly disturbances we had experienced occurred within a ten-minute window of time, between 3:00 a.m. and 3:10 a.m. What better way to get our attention than by constantly awakening us in the middle of the night? We had been disturbed by smoke detectors, footsteps, strange appearances, and the melodies of the glass globes. It seemed that interrupting our sleep had been the main objective of those incidences.

It did not make sense to me that there should be a long period when nothing unusual occurred, followed by a renewal of such activity. But whether the appearance of the nail had been an isolated occurrence or if things were going to begin anew would soon become clear.

One evening, shortly after I had found the nail, I lit a tea candle in a decorative glass holder. The holder sat upon a small table beside an antique rocking chair in the living room, and the flicker of the candle light etched the image of the decorative glass against the nearby corner walls. We all thought the effect was pretty, especially Rosa, who delighted in watching it. The candle was small, and if left to burn, would have lasted only a short period of time. About an hour after lighting it and several hours before bed time, I blew out the flame. As a further precaution, I glanced into the holder before I went upstairs that night to ensure the candle had been completely extinguished.

Late the next morning I folded laundry in the living room, occasionally glancing at the television, while Rosa finger-painted a colourful creation in the family room. When lunch time approached, I saw Kammie and Matt racing up to the front porch for their break from school. I picked up the last pair of socks, turned off the television, and went to the front door to greet them. Matt was very excited because he had brought home a Magic-Eye three-dimensional book from the library and was eager to show it to me.

As I carried a platter of sandwiches from the kitchen to the dining room table, a bright light in the far corner of the living room caught my eye and I turned towards it. The candle holder was glowing brilliantly, and its images were dancing around the walls. All three children were in the family room, and Kammie and Matt had not been in the living room since they had come home for lunch. None of them would have lighted that candle anyway; they all knew they were not allowed to play with matches, which were kept in a high cupboard out of reach.

I stood amid the piles of recently folded laundry and watched as the candle's flame jumped about erratically inside its glass container. I knew the candle had not been burning since the evening before. Not only was it impossible for the small tea candle to have blazed for that long, but it had not been burning while I had folded clothes that morning only a few feet away. The fact that the candle had seemed to ignite by itself was disturbing enough, but the intensity of the flame it produced was really alarming. I blew out the candle, carried the holder into the kitchen, and doused the candle's waxy remains in a cup of cold water to make certain it was no longer flammable. Then I threw it away.

Kammie was with the dog out in the backyard and I was at the refrigerator getting some milk when I heard Matt call for me from the dining room. "Just a minute," I answered, and poured milk into three small glasses.

Again I heard him call, this time a bit more urgently. I walked to the dining room doorway and waited to hear what he wanted, but he did not look up from his Magic-Eye book.

"What did you want?" I asked.

"I didn't want anything," he said.

"You just called me twice, when I was in the kitchen," I reminded him.

Matt slowly shook his head and looked sincerely puzzled.

"I heard you call Mommy too. It was your voice," said Rosa, coming into the dining room.

"I didn't hear anything," said Matt, going back to his book.

Rosa and I looked at each other and shrugged our shoulders. We had both heard a little boy call for his mother, and we had both assumed it had been Matt in the next room. No windows were open to let in a voice from outside, and it had definitely seemed to come from the dining room where my son was sitting. When Kammie came back into the house, I asked her if she had been the one who had called me, but she shook her head. And, in answer to my next question, she informed me that she had not heard anyone calling for their mother. So, as Matt insisted that he had not spoken, we dropped the matter and went on with our lunch.

While we ate, Matt peeked at his book, trying to make the hidden pictures in it appear to him in three dimensions. He was growing frustrated because he could not quite figure out how to make it work. He was so engrossed in the book that he accidentally knocked his glass of milk off of the table and onto his lap. I took the book away, mopped up the mess on the floor, and told him to go upstairs and quickly change into clean clothes. As Kammie was already finished with her lunch, she went upstairs along with Matt to brush her teeth and get ready to return to school for the afternoon.

Rosa was busy colouring a picture in the living room, seated at a little table-and-chair set just inside the opened doors that led in from the foyer. I was putting the lunch dishes into the kitchen sink when I heard a loud commotion on the stairs. Glancing down the hallway that ran from the kitchen to the foyer, I saw a small blond-haired boy dressed in gray leap off of the stairway, run across the foyer floor, and then rush into the living room. Piper, asleep in the kitchen, bolted up at the loud noise and dashed excitedly towards the child, wanting to play with him. I impatiently hurried down the hall because there was no doubt in my mind that Matt had just raced into the living room when he was supposed to be getting changed for school. I was also forever warning them not to run on the stairs.

77

Rosa, who was still colouring, looked up in surprise when I hurried into the room.

"Where did Matt go?" I asked her, quickly looking around the living room.

"He isn't in here," she said.

"Rosa," I replied, "I saw him run in here two seconds ago. We don't have time for games; the kids are going to be late for school. Where did he go?"

Piper was now sniffing around the room and whining, as if she were still looking for the boy, too.

"Just you came in, Mommy," Rosa said, looking at me with confusion.

It had only taken a few seconds for me to reach the living room doorway, but by the time I got into the room, the child had completely vanished. There was no way he could have left the living room without my seeing him.

"Matt!" I called out impatiently. "Where are you?"

I heard a small voice answer me from upstairs in Matt's bedroom.

"I'm up here," he said.

When I looked at Rosa in surprise, she smiled at me and nodded her head in an "I told you so" sort of way.

"Are you dressed yet?" I called, knowing he could not possibly have finished changing his clothes if he really had just run across the foyer.

"Yes," he called. "And I've brushed my teeth too."

Kammie was a few inches taller than Matt. Her hair was a bit darker and quite long, and she had been wearing a red outfit that day. Still I reasoned that, since there were only the four of us in the house, it must have been Kammie I had seen instead of Matt.

"Was it Kammie who came in here just before me?" I asked Rosa. She shook her head and continued to colour her picture, unaware of my bewilderment. Given the speed at which that child had rushed through the doorway, he would have run right into Rosa's chair and table, and yet she had been oblivious to anyone except me entering the room.

"Kammie?" I called.

"I'm up in the bathroom brushing my teeth," my oldest daughter called down from the second floor.

Matt came down the stairs at a safe pace, dressed in jeans and a green sweater, and started to put on his boots.

"Did you want me?" he asked.

"No, I just didn't know where you were," I said, trying to make sense out of what had just happened so I could convince myself I was not losing my mind.

"I went up to get changed like you told me to," he said, petting Piper who was now nuzzling up against him.

"I know. You're a good boy." I forced myself to smile but noticed my hands were shaking as I opened up the front door. When Kammie came down the stairs, they both headed back to school.

I walked into the kitchen and picked up the phone, feeling the need to talk to another adult about what had just happened. I called Ted on his cellular phone and caught him as he sat in a lineup at a drive-through restaurant. He was having lunch on the road as his out-of-town meeting with a client had run longer than expected.

I told Ted about seeing the young boy run across the foyer.

"Do you want me to come home?" he asked, thinking I was frightened.

"No, I'm okay," I answered, and was surprised to find that I actually was.

The fact that the presence was that of a small boy made that sighting different. It made me feel more sad than frightened that this child, who was perhaps even younger than Matt, was a presence in our home. The energy and rambunctious nature the young boy had manifested were just like those of any other youngster. I found nothing terrifying or threatening about him; he was apparently only the spirit of a child who was now no longer alive.

Sighting the boy was also much less scary, not only because it had taken place in daylight, but because he had not attempted to communicate or interact with anyone in the house. Matt and Kammie had not been aware of him on the second floor where I assumed he must have been before running down the stairway. And obviously Rosa had not seen him enter the living room. He had not seemed to notice that the dog and I were right behind him after he ran through the foyer, but both Piper and I had been very aware of his presence.

After the children were tucked into their beds that night, I turned on the lullaby tape I played for them at bed time. They fell asleep every evening to the soft music coming from the cassette player in the hallway. We all said our goodnights, and I was headed back down the stairs when the machine suddenly clicked off. The lullaby tape signified the end of play and the beginning of sleep time, so I thought perhaps Kammie was playfully showing me that she did not yet want to go to bed. I was a bit surprised, though, that she had been able to press the stiff button on the fairly old cassette player firmly enough to stop the tape.

"That's not funny," I said as I turned to head back upstairs. I fully expected to see Kammie smiling impishly beside the machine, but she was still snuggled in her bed where I had left her only moments before. There was no way she could have got back into bed that quickly without my seeing or hearing her.

"Who turned this off?" I asked, after looking at the cassette player. The play button had disengaged when the stop button had been pushed down.

All three children peered out of their beds at me in the hallway and shrugged.

"I didn't," they all said.

The cassette player had always worked reliably. I turned the tape on again and listened to the music play for several seconds. After convincing myself that I had put the tape in incorrectly or had not pushed the start button hard enough the last time, I started back downstairs, leaving the music behind me.

As I reached the foyer at the bottom of the stairs, I heard another loud click and the music again stopped playing. I raced up the stairs and found the hallway empty but the machine had been turned off once more. The children all looked at me in wonderment, and I hid my uneasy feeling so they would not be frightened. Twice more I left the cassette playing, and both times the machine clicked off as soon as I was halfway down the stairs.

"Why is it doing that?" Kammie asked.

"Maybe it doesn't want it to be bed time," Matt laughed.

He had been jokingly referring to the machine, but when I heard that innocent remark, I felt goose bumps rise all over my body and I shuddered slightly. I thought of the child I had seen earlier in the day. That was just the sort of thing a rambunctious little boy might do to try to delay going to bed.

I rewound the tape to the beginning of the lullaby and said in a soft but firm voice, "That's enough, now." The cassette player worked perfectly after that.

That night, however, for the first time in a long while, we were jarred awake at three o'clock in the morning by a smoke detector sounding its alarm. Both Ted and I were more tired than frightened, and more frustrated than angry. Yet the jolt it gave us was still upsetting.

The next morning, after everyone else had left for the day, Rosa and I finished up our breakfast in the new family room. With its large windows and southern exposure, that room was the brightest in the house, and we spent a lot of time there. I would often put a CD on, and Rosa would dance around the room, song after song.

As I washed up the breakfast dishes in the adjacent kitchen, Rosa asked if I would put on the soundtrack from the movie *Michael*. We had recently watched that film, which was about an angel. She loved to dance to those songs, and when her favourite, "Spirit in the Sky," came on, I went into the family room and danced with her. We laughed and spun each other around. When the song was over, Rosa asked if we could dance to it once more before we ran an errand and the other children came home for lunch. I programmed the CD to play the eleventh song, "Spirit in the Sky," and again we laughed and danced along with the music.

When the song had finished playing, I turned off the stereo and asked Rosa to go to the bathroom and brush her teeth so we could go. I finished up in the kitchen, and just as I was about to lock the back door in the family room, I heard a click from the stereo in the opposite corner. Its monitor lights came on and "Spirit in the Sky" began to blare through the speakers at a much louder volume than before. This shocked me so much that it took a few seconds to even react.

Rosa, of course, rushed out of the bathroom, happily thinking I had turned the stereo on again so we could do some more dancing.

"Good," she said. "I wanted to dance some more too, Mommy."

I walked over to the stereo and turned down the volume. I knew I had turned it off. Rosa could not have touched it because she had been in the bathroom, and she and I were the only two in the house. If I had somehow caused it to turn back on accidentally, there was still no way I could have made it immediately start playing "Spirit in the Sky" as it had. That title was number eleven and the machine was programmed to automatically begin at the first song, no matter at what point on the CD it had been when it was turned off. And besides, I had not even been near it.

I thought again of the small blond boy I had seen the previous day. Perhaps that was his way of letting me know he wanted the dancing and laughter to continue. Maybe he enjoyed that song as much as Rosa did.

9

THE YOUNG GIRL

A few weeks later, in the middle of a very cold February, Rosa looked out the living room window and excitedly reported that there was a little dog on our porch. I looked out to see a tiny white poodle sniffing around one of the pillars near our front door, shivering uncontrollably. I could see it was not wearing a collar, and I did not recognize if from our neighbourhood.

I opened the front door to try to persuade the dog to come inside until I could find its owner, but the noise frightened it. The poor little animal ran down the front steps of the porch and along the snowy street. Rosa and I slipped on our boots and coats and followed the poodle down the road to where it was huddled against a neighbour's parked car. It shivered as much from fear as cold, and when I kneeled down, it leaped into my arms and buried its snowy face in my warm winter coat.

I carried the poodle back to our house, and after shutting Piper in another room, put it down in the foyer. After we had removed our boots and hung up our coats, Rosa decided the dog needed a name and thought "Snowflake" would be perfect. She was white, and we had found her in the snow. I explained to Rosa that we could only keep this little dog until we found its real owners, but I could tell she was already becoming attached to it.

The telephone rang and I went to answer it, leaving Rosa alone with our new little friend. It was Ted calling, and I told him about the little white poodle. I also informed him that, after we had finished our conversation, I was going to call the local radio station and ask them to mention Snowflake on their afternoon Lost and Found program. The little dog had obviously been well cared for and its owners were probably worried. After I had made that call, I put some food and water into dishes and placed them on the kitchen floor. As I walked back into the foyer to get the dog, I heard Rosa roaring with laughter.

"What's so funny?" I called out. "Where have you two gone?"

"We're up here!" Rosa shouted from the second floor. "Snowflake knows how to go up the stairs!"

I immediately understood my daughter's amazement. Piper refused to go up the stairs, and my little girl had not seen a dog do that in this house.

When I reached the second floor, I found Rosa and the dog in the master bedroom. Rosa was laughing and excitedly pointing at Snowflake, but I felt uneasy when I saw what the little dog was doing. It had jumped up on our bed and climbed over onto Ted's bedside table. It stood upon it on its two back legs, determinedly batting its front paws at some unseen object above its head. The poodle was totally oblivious to us and kept its eyes fixed on one particular spot in the air.

"What is Snowflake doing?" Rosa again laughed.

"I don't know. Isn't she silly?" I tried to laugh too before I picked up the little animal and carried it back down the stairs.

The moment I placed the poodle on the floor, it bolted from my arms and raced up the stairs again. I could not believe how fast a dog that small could run. In the blink of an eye it was at the top of the stairs, and by the time Rosa and I had reached the second floor hallway, Snowflake was already back on the bedside table, swatting into the air, and fixedly staring at the same spot as before.

I again carried her out of the bedroom and, this time, closed the door. When I released Snowflake in the foyer, the poodle raced up the stairs and started to whine and bark and scratch at the master bedroom door. The little dog was frantic to get back inside the bedroom, and she refused to leave the door for the remainder of her short stay.

Back downstairs I spotted a car slowly circling the neighbourhood. After it drove by a second time, I went out and asked the man, woman, and small child in the car if they were looking for a lost dog. They described their poodle to me, and I realized they were Snowflake's owners. The radio station had promised to mention the poodle on their Lost and Found segment but that would not be for another hour. It was wonderful luck to have found its owners so quickly. Rosa, however, was sorry to see the poodle go and sadly waved goodbye as the car drove away.

Later that day I re-opened our bedroom door. I felt uncomfortable when I remembered how strangely the little dog had acted towards something it apparently could see hovering between the closet door and our bed. Unlike Piper, who refused to even climb the stairs, the little poodle had frantically tried to reach whatever it sensed there. The claw marks it had left on the outside of the door were a permanent reminder of that.

By the end of March everything seemed calm in our house again. The nights had been so peaceful that, for a few weeks, we were able to sleep for a full eight hours without any interruption. But that calm did not last.

One night, after everyone was sleeping soundly, I awakened with a jolt. I did not know what it was that had disturbed me because I had not been dreaming and did not hear any noises within the house. I was on my left side, facing the window, with my back towards Ted. I lay for a few moments, wide awake in the glow from the children's nightlights shining in from the hallway, trying to get back to sleep, and decided to shift my position to get more comfortable. As I rolled over, I saw someone at Ted's side of the bed looking at him, and realized immediately it was not one of our children. I was shocked to see a spirit, but was not as terrified as I had been when I had seen the tall woman in the cape and veil.

Although it was alarming to have her so close, I could see that she was only a young girl, of about thirteen, from the turn of the century or perhaps an even earlier time. Her image was so clear that each blonde strand of hair on her young head was visible, and I thought it looked oddly dry and frizzy. I was fascinated by the appearance of that child in full, vivid colour. I had pored over countless old photographs that captured the images of people from long ago, but they were always in black and white or brownish tones. Seeing that girl as she had appeared in life was astonishing, even if only from that perspective. Her hair was so light in colour it was almost platinum. It hung down loose to her shoulders, but the front sections were pulled back by a piece of white material, which was tied behind her head in a large bow.

THE YOUNG GIRL

Her clothing was worn in several layers. Over a loose-fitting dress in dusty rose or lavender, she wore a white apron, or pinafore, with small ruffles around the shoulders that appeared to be of the same material as the bow in her hair. I could see each fiber in the fabric's weave as I stared at the slightly transparent image of the girl. She appeared to be as real and solid as any person, yet I could still see the closet door and wall behind her. Light seemed to emanate from and glow around her form.

I felt a mixture of fright and amazement. Although it seemed impossible, the very real and definite image of a Victorian-era teenaged girl stood only a few feet from me. It was not my eyes playing tricks or the result of an overactive imagination or a dream. Nor was the image fleeting; it remained in place long enough for me to study her appearance closely.

The girl continued to stare down at Ted as he slept soundly, intent on studying his facial features just as I had been examining her. Feeling protective towards him, I slowly inched across the bed and draped myself over his back and side without attracting her attention. If he awoke and saw her right above him, only a few inches from his face, he would be terrified, and I did not want my husband to suffer a heart attack. The very idea of him finally seeing a spirit and the fear it would cause him after all his skepticism suddenly struck me as comical, and I almost let out a nervous and somewhat hysterical giggle.

By moving closer to Ted, I also hoped to be able to see her face. In my former position, I had only been able to see her profile, and the tall woman whose form had loomed in our bedroom doorway had seemed to have no face at all. The longer the girl's image stayed before me, the less frightened I became, and the more awe I felt at what I was seeing.

The girl continued to inch closer towards Ted, and it seemed as if she might reach out her hand to touch his face at any moment. I now wanted to awaken Ted so that he could share that incredible experience with me, but any abrupt motion might have caused the girl to disappear. I pushed his back gently with my hand to rouse him. That movement, though subtle, alerted the girl to my watching her, and she slowly turned and looked right at me for several seconds with a blend of frustration and irritation. I was so astonished that I froze. She was obviously unhappy that I had disturbed her while she was contentedly watching my husband sleep. She turned her eyes back to Ted and gave him one long last look. Then she once again glared at me before she turned to go.

The girl's obvious irritation terrified me. The look she had given me made me feel as if I was an intruder in my own home. Although she had exhibited a strong curiosity towards Ted, her response to me when I had interrupted her observation of him had been clearly one of annoyance.

In a calmer and more rational moment I might have realized that her frustrated reaction was similar to that of any modern-day teenager. But I was far from calm; I was unnerved by the fact that she had become aware of my presence, acknowledged it, and then interacted with me. Had she turned to me and smiled instead of grimaced, I probably would have felt a similar sense of panic.

The girl did not disappear immediately. I watched with fascination as her seemingly solid form dissipated into tiny particles of light that danced in front of me for a few brief moments. Mesmerized, I forgot my fear and leaned over Ted and swiped at the tiny glimmering orbs. That movement caused them to bounce about even more animatedly until, one by one, they vanished altogether.

Ted continued to sleep while I lay wide awake for the rest of the night, thinking about what I had seen. In all honesty, the experience had completely unnerved me. I knew without a doubt that I had seen a spirit. Although I knew that the two other spirits I had seen were also real, neither of them had made me feel that we were the intruders. They had behaved mischievously and their actions had often been startling, but I did not believe they harboured malignant feelings towards us. Now that the girl had expressed her annoyance with my presence, I no longer felt comfortable living in the house. Although she had not expressed hostility or hatred, her irritation made me feel vulnerable.

It was not until the following morning, before Kammie, Matt, and Rosa were awake, that I mentioned the events of the night to Ted. While we shared an early breakfast, I told him that I wanted to seriously discuss moving from the house. Ted assured me that, although he knew I believed I had seen ghosts in the house, he wished he had seen something. Surely, he argued, there had to be some plausible reason for it all.

"Call me the next time you see anything," he told me. "I just have to see it for myself."

Later that day, Ted, Kammie, Matt, and Rosa relaxed in the family room while I prepared dinner in the adjoining kitchen. While chopping vegetables on the cutting board, I saw the light in the foyer come on at the front of the house. I turned slowly to look at the light, knowing everyone else in the family was in the other room and could not possibly have touched the hall switch. As I stared at the light, it turned off again.

"Ted..." I called.

"Yeah?" he answered.

"Could you come here, please?" I asked, not wanting to scare the children.

"What is it?" he persisted.

Finally I caught his eye, and when he saw the look on my face, he realized why I had called him. As I waited for Ted to walk into the kitchen so he too would be able to see into the foyer, the light went on and off again four times. By the time he was by my side, however, the foyer was again dark and the light remained off. Frustrated, I told him what had happened. After watching the light for a moment, he shrugged and went back into the family room.

10

INVESTIGATING THE PARANORMAL

The worst part about dealing with the haunting in our house for me was feeling there was no one to turn to for guidance or moral support. Although a few immediate family members and one close friend knew what was happening, I did not discuss it with anyone else. I was afraid people might think I was hallucinating, crazy, or both.

After the appearance of the young girl's spirit, I decided to do a search on the Internet for information that pertained to what we were dealing with in our home. I hoped I might be able to locate an organization that could advise me on what to do.

I was surprised to find so many sites dealing with the paranormal, and as I researched a few, I learned there were different types of hauntings. In many cases what seemed to be a ghost was actually a phenomenon called a residual haunting, which left a psychic impression in one particular location. That was created by an event that had caused terrible emotional stress, such as a murder or violent death. This event seemed to repeat itself over and over again like a clip from a movie. I found it difficult to understand fully how this was possible, but it was evidently reported fairly often.

Residual hauntings could also result in a certain smell, noise, or other stimulus in a particular area due to its frequency at an earlier time. Rather than being caused by a tragedy, it was merely the continuation of something that had once happened repeatedly in that location.

If it were a residual haunting from a psychic impression, rather than a real entity causing the phenomenon, then there was no direct conscious contact with any living person who witnessed the occurrence. While they might very well have seen or heard the impression of what they assumed was a ghost, the entity was not at all aware of their presence and did not acknowledge them.

What I had read concerning residual haunting made me think of the footsteps we all heard so often on the main stairway in our home. Those seemed to be a perfect example of a noise resulting from a psychic impression left in a particular area due to earlier repetition. Residual haunting could even explain the smell of the wood-burning cook stove and the aroma of baking that so often seemed to come from our kitchen.

The more I researched, however, the more I realized that we were also dealing with spirits that very definitely interacted with us. They made direct eye contact, changed their facial expressions, and even waved greetings. Those conscious gestures had been made directly to us in an attempt to communicate.

As I explored the various material available on the Internet, I located the website of a paranormal society, an association that seemed to have a lot of experience with haunted houses. Listed on a page at that site were the common signs of a haunting. A brief statement following the list urged the reader to contact the site's author if they had experienced any one of those several signs, which ranged from hearing footsteps, to having household lights or appliances turn off or on, to actually seeing shadows or apparitions. Not only had we experienced every one of the itemized signs, but we had also witnessed many more that were not included in the list.

I sat at the computer and prepared to write a long e-mail message to the paranormal investigator explaining what had happened in our home and asking for any possible advice on how to stop it. But as I attempted to type out the letter containing details of the various sightings and our other haunting experiences, the keyboard suddenly seemed to have a mind of its own. At first I was just frustrated that I could not complete the message and send it, but I gradually began to feel frightened. At times the keyboard would simply freeze and I could not type at all. Or I would be able to type the words but then the screen would go blank and my entire email would be erased. Typing my message proved impossible. In frustration, I turned off the computer. I planned to leave it for a while and try again later.

The following Saturday, while Ted was in the backyard playing with the children, I again attempted to type my message. That time I was successful and managed to explain everything that had happened in considerable detail, including the difficulty I had had in sending out the first message. The next day I received a reply to my e-mail from Rhonda Twine, a psychic paranormal investigator.

The reply from Rhonda was helpful in many ways, not least of which was that I now had someone with whom I could rationally discuss the situation. She had been helping people in similar circumstances for some time and was very encouraging in her hope that it was possible to return our household back to normal.

In response to my mentioning the strange attraction we had initially felt to the house, Rhonda said she sensed that perhaps the spirits had wanted us to come and live there to be of help to them in some way. Regarding our pet's refusal to go up the stairway to the second floor, and especially into Matt's bedroom, Rhonda mentioned that animals were very sensitive to energies other than human, and this would account for the dog's behaviour. She felt there was very likely a portal, or an entry point for the spirits to come and go, located somewhere near the attic or the stairway leading to it. I remembered how the attic and Matt's room appeared to have been closed off before we purchased the property and how it was almost impossible at times to keep that area of the house heated properly.

When I described my sighting of the woman in a cape and headdress in the bedroom doorway, I told Rhonda I had been frozen with fear. She asked me if I meant that I had been unable to move at all, if there been any pressure on my chest, and if I had heard noises in the room. I did not recall feeling physically restrained. I had been so afraid of the vision, it was as if time stood still, but nothing had seemed to keep me from moving other than my own fear. Rhonda told me of a phenomenon called Phantomania or Old Hag Syndrome in which you felt as though something was sitting on your chest, pinning you down. I was relieved that had not been my experience. I had not felt that anything was trying to intentionally terrify or harm me.

Rhonda cautioned me that emitting fear or anger in the presence of a spirit gave the entity more energy to manifest. Although, both feelings were natural responses to the presence of a spiritual intruder in one's home, I hoped I could control my feelings better in the future.

Rhonda encouraged my use of religious items in the house, particularly in the children's bedrooms, and I was glad I had hung up the cross and angel pictures. It made me feel better knowing they were there.

She told me that, because the spirits could see and hear everything, it was important to speak aloud to them to open up lines of communication. Perhaps, I thought, that alone could help settle the spirits and convince them to leave. However, Rhonda felt that, since at least two of the spirits appeared to be children, the haunting may have been quite involved. Why would they be earthbound and so attached to that particular setting?

She felt there was a direct correlation between the new family room being added onto the existing house and the experiences we were having in our home. She sensed that the addition was upsetting to them because perhaps the building itself was now covering something of importance under the ground on the property, something they did not want concealed. The fact that a woman, a little boy, and an adolescent girl had all been clearly seen did not surprise Rhonda, because as she explained to me in her letter, where there is one spirit, there are usually more.

In our correspondence I asked Rhonda about the significance of the smoke detectors going off so frequently in the middle of the night. She said that, since it did not seem to be difficult for spiritual entities to manipulate electrical objects, a smoke detector would be a likely target for such activity. As they were set off only when the family was asleep, a reaction of fear and annoyance was assured, thereby giving them more energy to incarnate. I had thought of those disturbances as random, harmless acts, but I now saw them from a different perspective.

Rhonda wondered if the house had ever been a hospital. I had researched the property's records extensively, and to my knowledge, it had always been a single family residence. That did not help to explain the presence of the woman both Matt and I had sighted, whom I was sure had been a nurse. Rhonda felt that the little boy and young girl may have been under the nurse's care and had died there from an epidemic or some other such tragedy. The woman might therefore still think she must watch over them in that spot. That could perhaps have happened before the present house had been built on the same piece of land, she suggested.

I thought it was entirely possible that the land had been inhabited while it was still Crown land. Prior to its purchase by F. Lincoln in 1865, who had probably used it as farmland, a family may have lived on it as "squatters." As they were not the legal property owner, their name would not have been recorded in the land registry books.

Rhonda seemed most concerned about whether there had been a fire on the property and thought that might definitely account for the constant manipulation of the smoke detectors. However, there was no evidence that the house itself had ever sustained damage from a fire, and our neighbour Donelle had not mentioned such a tragedy taking place.

I finally asked Rhonda if she knew of any paranormal investigators who lived fairly close to our home. She admitted that she could not recommend anyone in our remote area of the country, but based on all the evidence I had given her, she would be willing to make the long trip to our town herself. As tempting as her offer was, we really could not afford to pay for her extensive travel expenses. Rhonda understood about the monetary restraint and offered to keep in touch with me through e-mail. We could continue to work together and hopefully figure out a way to make our home, and lives, ordinary again.

11

OUT OF CONTROL

I felt greatly relieved that I now had Rhonda, with whom to corre-
spond, because she understood the situation we were facing in
our house. I had found our contact therapeutic, yet the unusual
activity had escalated and was now occurring on an almost daily
basis. Items began to disappear, vanishing altogether or showing up
again in such unlikely spots that we could not figure out how they
could possibly have been placed there. No item of real monetary or
sentimental value was ever lost, such as a wallet or jewelry, but
cooking utensils, books, clothing, and especially the children's toys
would be there one minute and missing the next. They would
remain lost for days or even weeks, only to show up on top of a high
shelf in a closet or under the stairs in the basement.

As those articles went missing, however, the children began to find coins throughout the house in equally strange locations. That phenomenon, which had started on our first day in the house, had continued, although the coins had never appeared in that same large quantity. Ted and I had never given the matter a great deal of thought. Certainly people did drop coins now and again, so it was not unreasonable to assume the money had come from one of our own pockets. When added to all the other incidents, though, the frequency of the coins' appearance and the locations in which they were found finally caught my attention.

We also experienced a problem with all the clocks in the house. No matter how often I would replace the batteries, it was impossible to keep them running consistently for any length of time. Even the few that were plugged into outlets would stop for long periods, for no apparent reason.

Watches were also affected. My gold wristwatch, which had been a gift from Ted the previous Christmas, quit working one afternoon at 2:30 p.m. Replacing the battery did not restore it to working order, so I put it in a desk drawer and later bought another cheaper watch. That one stopped working at 7:00 a.m., within a couple of days, even though the sales lady had installed a new battery when I had purchased it.

I planned to take both watches to a jeweler the next day to see if they could be fixed. When I opened the desk drawer to retrieve the gold one, I found it was now not only working properly but was somehow even set to the correct time. Puzzled by this, but relieved to have it working again, I put the recently purchased but seemingly broken one into the desk drawer. A few days later, I opened the drawer and saw that it too was not only working again but was set to the correct time.

Our nights were fraught with an increasing number of disturbances. After we were in bed, we could often hear loud knocks in the house. It was difficult, though, to determine from where the noise was originating. The sound had a rapping quality, as if someone were knocking on a door to gain entry, yet it seemed to resonate throughout the walls.

On a number of occasions, just as I was dozing off to sleep, a drop of cold liquid I assumed was water splashed on my hand, abruptly rousing me. I would lay wide awake in the still of the night wiping the wetness off my skin as my husband slept peacefully beside me. I found those incidents more strange than frightening. Certainly the liquid I wiped off my hand was real enough, yet I could not explain how or why it had come to be there.

On many nights my sleep was interrupted by the strange sensation of having my face, and especially my nose, tickled with a fluffy object such as a feather or a piece of lace. I was not terrified by that and could appreciate, at times, the comic element of the gentle playfulness. However, I could not help but become annoyed when it was so often repeated, and affected my sleep. I reminded myself not to show anger or fear and thereby further energize the entity who was tickling me. And, when I ignored the sensation rather than growing upset, it did become less frequent and less intense.

Aside from the sighting of spirits, the most frightening occurrence I experienced in the night was the sensation of being touched. Once the feel of a very heavy, cold hand on my arm awakened me. I knew it could not be Ted, as he was turned away from me, and the surprising weight and chill of that hand did not resemble his touch. The sensation of having my arm gently gripped lasted for several seconds, long enough for me to notice that, although it was so heavy, the actual size of the hand was quite small. Even when I could no longer sense the weight of the hand upon me, the coldness of its touch against my skin remained for a long time.

I awakened another night to feel someone gently running their fingers through my hair. I felt a hand brush the locks away from my closed eyes and tuck them carefully behind my ear. From the angle of the hand's touch I knew that someone was standing over me, and I reached up, assuming it was my husband. But no one was there. When I opened my eyes, I saw that Ted was sound asleep with his back towards me, and it had not been him at all.

In my next e-mail message to Rhonda, I mentioned that the haunting activity persisted and actually seemed to be increasing. I had taken her previous advice and frequently spoke aloud to any unseen listeners, explaining that our family did not want to be frightened by their presence. That had had little effect on the strange occurrences, however, and I was starting to feel convinced that the only way to remove ourselves from that bizarre paranormal situation was to remove ourselves from the house.

12

FINDING A KEY

Rhonda responded immediately to my e-mail, in which my desperation had been clear. She had gone back to my original letter and carefully read it over once more, seeking more insight into the case. The activity had increased alarmingly when we had built onto the existing house, that much was clear. But she wondered if that was the only thing that had triggered those disturbances; she felt there had to be more to it. When she re-read a particular paragraph in my original letter, she thought it might hold the key to many of the problems we were experiencing. In the paragraph to which Rhonda was referring, I had mentioned the items Stuart had unearthed in the backyard as he dug the footing holes for the addition onto the house. Rhonda asked me for more details on that.

The increase in unusual activity had certainly occurred when the new room was being added onto the house. Since the footings had been dug at the very start of the project, perhaps it had been the disturbance and subsequent removal of those objects that had triggered that phenomena and not just the construction that followed.

In a long e-mail message, I described exactly what had been found when the construction began the previous spring. I told her how the builder had been deepening the holes in the back-yard to about five feet in depth for the footings, which would support the cement piers for the new room. I described the items that had been found: a small, perfectly preserved white glass jar that had probably contained some kind of cosmetic or skin cream at least a century ago; a small and even older clay ink-well, in good condition, that must have been buried in that spot for several generations; and a very old glass button that looked like it might once have adorned a young girl's dress or coat. I told her that all of those items had been given to Kammie, who displayed them on the window sill in her bedroom.

On the day I received Rhonda's response, I was busy nursing the three children back to health from a stomach virus. Kammie had been the first to get sick and had almost recovered from it when the two younger ones starting showing the same symptoms. All three were confined to their beds, and I went from room to room tending to them. There was an out-of-town family reunion that weekend, and I was anxious to have everyone feeling better so we would not have to miss it.

When I found a moment, I checked my e-mail and found Rhonda's message. Given what I had described to her, she felt strongly that I should immediately remove the items from the house that had been unearthed and replace them where they had been originally found. She explained to me that maybe those small things had had a very special significance to someone a long time ago, and perhaps they did not want them taken from the spot where they had been lying undisturbed for all those years.

As a parent, it was not difficult to understand why three such seemingly insignificant objects could be that important to someone. I knew how much my own daughter admired them, and I could see that another little girl might have treasured those items and felt that no one should have possession of them but her. In a time when children had so few possessions when compared with today, those small things could have been the child's most prized belongings.

I agreed with Rhonda that the best thing to do would be to place the items back where they had been found. The problem I had before me was explaining to Kammie why she had to part with them. She had witnessed the "bonker" lamp turning itself on and off, and had heard the footsteps on the stairs, the knocking in the walls, and her glass globes break into melody in the night. She had claimed to see her china doll move as if manipulated. But Kammie had never heard us discuss the fact that spirits could possibly be causing all of those disturbances.

I went into her room and sat beside Kammie on the bed.

"Do you know what I've been thinking?" I said. "I think that a long time ago, a little girl, like you, may have owned all those things we found in the backyard when the new room was being built."

Kammie nodded her head in agreement. She glanced over at the items on her window sill and smiled.

"Maybe we shouldn't have taken them from where that little girl left them," I continued.

"We didn't take them, Mommy. Stuart found them and gave them to me," Kammie reminded me.

"That's right. Do you remember exactly where he found them?" I wondered.

My little girl again nodded her head.

"Could you show me when you're feeling better?" I asked.

"Why?" Kammie wanted to know.

"I think we should put them back where they were found."

"Oh, do we have to, Mommy?" she asked with disappointment.

"I know you like them. But I think we should think of those things as still belonging to the little girl who left them there, and put them back. If we knew who owned something we found, we would give it back to them, wouldn't we?" I asked.

"Do you mean like if we found a wallet or something?" Kammie asked, trying to understand what I was saying.

"Yes. If we found something, and knew who owned it, we would make sure that person got it back, wouldn't we?"

Kammie agreed that we would.

"Well, we know someone left those things buried out there for a reason. And maybe it was important to them that their things stayed there," I said.

That seemed to make sense to Kammie, and she got out of bed, picked up the items, and handed them to me.

"I'm going to put these downstairs, and when you're feeling better, we'll go outside into the backyard together and you can show me exactly where Stuart found them and we'll put them back."

Kammie nodded in agreement but asked if I would take a photograph of them before they were buried back in the ground so she would have a keepsake. I smiled at my daughter as I tucked her back into bed, assured her I would do that for her, and left the room with the objects.

Carrying the delicate items carefully, I went down the stairs, through the family room, and out the back door. I put them on the outdoor stairway railing and leaned them safely against the wall so they would not fall. They were also protected from any gusts of wind that might swirl around the yard. I breathed a sigh of relief. Just having them out of the house made me feel better. I quickly snapped a picture of the items for Kammie before I headed back upstairs to the attic and the computer.

I was about to begin typing an answer to Rhonda's last message when I heard a commotion coming from the second floor.

"Kammie is out of bed!" Rosa called up to me, knowing they had all been told to stay tucked in and resting.

I called out to Kammie to get back under her covers.

"She went downstairs," Matt informed me from his bedroom below.

I sighed, got up and went in search of Kammie, expecting to find her in the living room watching television. Instead I saw her standing in the dining room, staring out the window into the backyard.

"What are you doing, honey?" I asked as I walked up behind her.

Kammie jumped when she felt my hand upon her arm and reeled around.

I was startled by her reaction.

"What's wrong?" I asked.

"I didn't know who was behind me. I didn't hear you coming," Kammie explained nervously.

"What are you doing down here? I told you to stay in bed," I reminded her.

"I know. I'm sorry. I just wanted to see where you put my things. I mean, the things we have to put back into the ground in the backyard," she replied.

"Did you see them?" I asked as I guided her back up the stairs to her room.

Kammie did not answer me, but I knew she would have had a clear view of the objects from the dining room window as it overlooked the back door and stairway landing. She remained unusually quiet as I tucked her into bed. I felt her forehead to see if her fever had risen and was glad to find that it had not. Still, she seemed pale, and I told her to get some rest.

As I left the room I looked back at Kammie with some concern. I wondered if removing the items from her room had upset her even more than I had expected. The expression she wore was more frightened than sad, and I was not quite sure what to think.

"Is everything all right?" I asked her from her doorway.

Kammie nodded but did not look at me, and I assumed she was unhappy because I took away her things.

"Sweetie, are you upset because we're putting everything back?" I asked.

"No," Kammie said firmly. "I don't want to see those things anymore."

That was an unexpected reply, but she had now closed her eyes. I left her to rest.

The following day the children were all feeling much better, and Matt and Kammie were able to return to school for the last day of the week. The next morning, we were going out of town for the family reunion, and the children were very excited.

That afternoon when they arrived home from school I asked Kammie if she wanted to show me the exact spot where the objects had been found in the backyard so we could put everything back in the ground. Although I had an idea as to where they had been found, having been called outside when the glass jar was discovered, I thought it might be important to Kammie to put them back herself.

"I don't think those things are there anymore," Kammie said quietly.

"Of course they are. Why wouldn't they be? I told you I would wait until you could help me," I reassured her.

"I think that girl took them," Kammie said.

"What girl?" I asked, even though her response had raised the hair on the back of my neck. I had never mentioned the apparition of the young girl that I had seen in the master bedroom to the children. As I waited for Kammie's reply, I hoped that she was talking about someone from the neighbourhood.

"Yesterday, when I got out of bed, I wanted to see where you put those things. So I went downstairs, and as I was walking through the dining room, I saw a girl through the window. She was standing outside the back door, looking at the things you put on the railing," she explained.

I stared quietly at my daughter for a moment. What she was saying was logically impossible. The gate to our backyard was kept locked at all times, and if anyone had even approached it, Piper would have barked a warning as she did when passersby strolled along the front sidewalk. The only possible entry into our backyard was through the house and out the back door.

"Why didn't you tell me someone was there?" I asked, while I tried to make sense of what she was saying.

"I thought you would be mad at me for getting out of bed and going downstairs when I was sick," Kammie explained with her child's logic.

"What did the girl look like?" I asked.

"She looked like she was playing dress-up in old fashioned clothes. She had blonde hair, and the front part of it was pulled into a big white bow at the back."

"How old was she?" I asked, feeling my knees starting to shake.

"She was tall, but she didn't look too old. I think she was maybe twelve or thirteen," Kammie said.

111

HAUNTED

I remained quiet for a moment, trying to think of what to say next.

"You don't believe me, do you?" she asked.

"Yes, I do," I assured her. "I do, I just want to know more about what she looked like so we can figure out who she was and how she got into our backyard. Have you ever seen her before?"

She shook her head.

"What colour was her dress?"

"Purple. And she had another white dress over top of that one."

She had described the girl that I had seen. The colour and style of her hair, and even her clothing, were exactly the same.

"What was she doing out there?" I asked, trying to get as much information out of Kammie as possible.

"She was just standing there looking at the things you put on the railing. Remember that feather I had in the ink-well?" she asked me.

I nodded. I had taken out the feather that Kammie had put in the ink-well when I had carried the items outside and took the photograph, but had then replaced it.

"She kept poking at that feather with her finger," Kammie told me.

"Did she look at you?" I asked, realizing that Kammie had stood only a few feet away from the girl. I hoped she had not given my daughter the same look of irritation she had given me.

"No, I don't think she saw me at all. She just kept looking at the things and poking at the feather."

Again I fell silent.

"I don't think you believe me. I did see her, Mommy, honest!" my daughter swore.

"I do believe you, sweetie," I told her.

"Are you sure?" Kammie asked, knowing the story sounded strange.

"Yes, because I've seen that girl too," I finally admitted to her.

"You have? When? Did you see her when you came down to get me?" she asked.

"No, I didn't. But I saw a girl that looks exactly like the one you described in my bedroom a few nights ago," I told her.

"What was she doing?" Kammie asked with a mixture of excitement and relief. She seemed happy to know I believed her.

"She was just watching Daddy sleeping," I said simply. I had no intention of telling her about the look the girl had given me or the fear I had felt.

Kammie seemed to find that funny, and giggled. I joined in with genuine laughter, remembering how I had almost done so when I had envisioned Ted's reaction to waking up and seeing her looking down at him.

"Who is she?" my daughter wanted to know.

"I don't know." I answered, still smiling and trying to remain cheerful.

"I bet she owns those things we found!" Kammie said, as though putting together an important puzzle piece.

"I bet she does too," I agreed.

"Can we go and see if everything is still there?" Kammie asked.

We went out the back door, and Kammie was happy to see that the jar, ink-well with feather, and button were exactly where I had placed them. No one had taken them after all.

Kammie and I went down the stairs and into the backyard. I walked over to the shed to get the shovel I would need to dig in the hard-packed dirt. I knew from my gardening that the soil's texture was almost like clay, and it would be difficult to dig deeply, but I was eager to bury the objects now that Kammie had also seen the girl's spirit.

"Mommy!" I heard my daughter call when I was inside the shed.

"I'll be there in a minute. I'm just getting the shovel," I called back.

"We don't need a shovel," she said.

"We'll need one to dig into that hard dirt," I reminded her.

"But they've already made a hole," Kammie said.

I came out of the shed when I heard that remark.

"What do you mean?" I asked her.

"Look," said Kammie, pointing at the ground. "It looks like they pushed a hole right into the ground exactly where Stuart found those things. This is where they want us to put them back."

As I approached the spot where Kammie was standing, I could only gasp and stare at the hole beside her that had indeed been "pushed" into the hard ground. Piper was not prone to digging holes in the yard, and there were no claw marks to indicate that she might have taken the notion to dig that one. Nor was there a pile of removed earth beside the hole. Rather, it appeared as if the ground had been shoved in by some unknown force to a depth of many inches, making a hole exactly the size needed to bury the items.

"Are you sure this is where Stuart found those things?" I asked, trying to hide my shock.

"Yes, I remember it was right here," Kammie said, still looking at the hole. "How did they do that?"

"I don't know," I answered truthfully.

I went to the top of the stairs and retrieved the items from the railing. I placed the jar in the bottom of the hole, with the button inside it. The ink-well went in next, with the feather by its side. Although it had not been found there, Kammie wanted to bury the feather because the girl she had seen poking at it seemed to like it. I then made several trips to the side garden for shovelfuls of loose soil to fill the hole. When everything was buried again, I returned the shovel to the shed. My daughter's small hand reached out for mine, and together we walked back into the house.

Some days later, Rosa and I were seated on the sofa in the living room reading a book together when Kammie and Matt returned from school and walked into the room to say hello.

"What's that?" Kammie asked me, pointing to the loveseat beside us. I looked over and saw an old piece of ribbon lying on a cushion. I assumed Rosa must had left it there earlier in the day, but when I picked it up, the material was stiff and brittle with age. As I looked at it more closely, I saw it was beautifully made with delicately woven golden threads. After determining that none of us had placed it on the cushion, I wondered if it were meant to be a small token of appreciation for our having put those items back in the ground. Kammie did not want it, but I appreciated it and used it as a bookmark for the journal I kept about our home.

13

THE WOMAN AT THE TREE

The night after Kammie and I had buried the objects back in the ground, all was peaceful in our home for a change and we awoke feeling rested. I dared to hope that the strange disturbances we had experienced were over.

Our weekend away at the family reunion was enjoyable and allowed us to forget about the house for awhile. When we returned, the house felt strangely empty of the strong presence I usually noticed upon entering it. I sensed a void in our home and was surprised not to feel comforted. I had hoped for the time when I no longer felt we were sharing our house. Now that whomever had been there appeared to have left, I was suprised to find that, although very relieved, I also felt a slight twinge of loss.

Perhaps the haunting really was over, simply because we had re-buried a few small objects in the yard.

After unpacking and resting from our long trip, I went up to the attic and began to write an e-mail message to Rhonda. I told her of our apparent success in ridding the house of its paranormal presence and thanked her for her help in the matter.

A few hours later, I received Rhonda's reply. She was not as optimistic as I that the spirits were really gone for good simply because we had given those objects back. She had suggested we do that and still thought it would be of some help, but she did not think that act alone would be enough to send the entities entirely on their way. She hoped that everything would settle back to normal for my family. If that turned out not to be the case, though, I could feel free to contact her if I wanted Rhonda and one of her colleagues to make the trip to our home to do a more in-depth investigation.

I dismissed her offer. Not only would it have been very costly for us, but I was confident that we finally had our house to ourselves.

The following week the two eldest children were back in school, and two of my friends came over for coffee one afternoon. Rosa sat beside me in the living room, facing our company and the foyer, while we chatted. Suddenly my little girl jumped a bit, as though startled. When I looked down at her, she smiled and nodded her head towards the hall. As the women continued to sip their coffee and talk about local events, Rosa and I watched as the foyer light turned itself off, then on, then off again, several times in a row. As I did not want my guests to be aware of that activity, I moved my seat over a bit, redirecting their gaze so that they would not detect the fluctuating light behind them with their peripheral vision.

Rosa started to giggle, as she found the light's activity quite amusing. Each time the light turned on, it would surprise her slightly and she would jump. Then she would chuckle with wonder when it turned itself off. When the women grew curious about what she found so entertaining out in the hallway, I decided it was time for her to go and play in the backyard.

I felt frustrated rather than frightened by that occurrence. Rhonda had been right. Burying those objects in the backyard had not been enough to stop the haunting altogether. It had seemed to quiet things down for a while, but apparently not for long and obviously not for good.

Several days later Kammie went over to a friend's house to play. When Ted and I went to pick her up, we visited for a few minutes with the Mullens. Because Amanda Mullen and Kammie had been best friends since preschool, we knew Amanda's parents, Beverly and Ray, fairly well. We stood outside and chatted with Beverly, who asked us how our trip to the reunion had been. We told her it had been wonderful.

"We drove by your house while you were gone," she mentioned. "I have to tell you about this really strange woman we saw on your front lawn."

I glanced over at Ted, who refused to acknowledge what she had said. He had made it clear to me that he did not want us to discuss our house's haunting with anyone in town. He was concerned we would be ridiculed for something he himself had trouble believing or understanding.

"What was she doing?" I asked casually.

"Well, we knew you were away, so when I saw her standing on your lawn as we drove by, I had Ray stop the van in front of the house just to see why she was standing there and what she was doing. We pulled up right near where she stood, but she didn't even seem to notice us. She just kept staring up at that huge weeping willow tree you have in your front yard."

"She was probably a neighbour," Ted said.

119

"No, I'm sure she wasn't. I didn't recognize her," Beverly told him. The Mullens, who only lived a few blocks from us, were life-long residents and knew most of the people in town.

"What did she look like?" Ted asked her.

"Really strange. She had on vintage clothing, and her hairstyle looked like it was from about a hundred years ago," she told us.

I looked at Ted, trying to read his thoughts. I did not think I should mention any of our experiences with the house, but I wanted Beverly to tell us more about the woman.

"What colour was her hair?" I asked.

"It was really blonde, almost white. And she was so tall, taller even than me," Beverly said, holding her hand several inches above her own height of five feet and ten inches.

"It must have just been a neighbour," Ted said again.

"Do you have any neighbours who dress like that? I've never seen any. And the weirdest part wasn't even how she looked, but how she acted. We were parked only a few feet away from her, but she didn't even turn her head to look at us. I don't think she even realized we were there. She never took her eyes off of that tree," Beverly said.

Not wanting to hear any more about the mystery woman in our yard, Ted went into the house to talk to Beverly's husband, Ray. After he left, Beverly looked at me quietly for a moment. "Have you ever met my sister, Dennise?" she finally asked me.

I shook my head.

"She's psychic. No one else in my family really believes in that kind of stuff, but she's made a believer out of me. She has this strong psychic ability, and she uses it all the time to help people."

I hesitated, not knowing what to say. I did not want to divulge too much about what we had been experiencing, but I was desperate to talk to someone like Dennise about our situation.

"I think there was something really strange about that woman we saw," she said again in a low voice. "I know this sounds weird, but I think maybe she was a spirit, or something like that, and she definitely seemed to be connected to your place."

I looked at Beverly and nodded my head. I could not bring myself to dismiss her account of what she had seen, and I wanted the opportunity to talk to Dennise. The spirit of the girl witnessed by both Kammie and I had been that of a thirteen-year-old, although her hair colour and clothing were similar to the woman Beverly had described. The "nurse" who had manifested in my bedroom had worn a headpiece and cloak, neither of which Beverly had mentioned. Perhaps what she had seen was another entity entirely.

"Would you like me to ask my sister to visit your house the next time she's in town? She could walk through it and tell you what she thinks," Beverly offered.

I quickly agreed. Although she lived fairly far away and would not be in town to visit for some time, Beverly promised she would discuss the matter with Dennise on the phone when they next spoke and let me know what was said. I felt very relieved. If there were so many spirits connected to our property, a psychic might be able to help us in dealing with them.

14

THE NEWSPAPERS

I cleared up the kitchen after breakfast as Ted, Kammie, and Matt headed out the front door to work and to school. Little Rosa waved to them from the living room window, and when they were finally out of sight, she joined me in the kitchen. As I turned to greet her, I saw the foyer light begin to switch on and off. I watched it for a few seconds, shrugged my shoulders with exasperation, and continued to load up the dishwasher. Rosa did not even acknowledge the blinking light as she wandered back to the living room, with Piper close behind.

It was a warm spring day, and the sun was streaming in through the windows of the kitchen and family room. I was just about to turn on the dishwasher when a pocket of cold, dense air passed right in front of me. I could actually feel it brush my nose, and I stood perfectly still, scarcely even breathing. The sensation passed within seconds, and the air around me reverted to normal room temperature. I was left standing in the warm kitchen with goose bumps all along my arms and legs and the tip of my nose still frigid.

I rushed into the living room to check on Rosa but found her engrossed in the cartoon show she was watching on television. She looked up at me when I came into the room.

"What's wrong?" she asked.

"Nothing," I said as calmly as possible. "I just wanted to see what you were up to."

"You look sad," my little daughter said with concern.

"No," I said and smiled. "I'm all right."

"That's good." Rosa smiled back at me and turned again to her program.

I stood in the living room for a few minutes, reluctant to return to the kitchen. The telephone's ring startled me, and I felt my heart racing as I picked up the receiver. It was our dentist's office calling to remind me that our six-month check-up was scheduled for the following afternoon. Just as I was about to thank the secretary for calling, the stereo in the family room came on, blaring music at full blast. The whole house seemed to reverberate with the noise. I ran into the family room with the portable phone, turned off the stereo, and apologized to her for the earsplitting racket.I was beginning to feel that whatever was sharing our house with us demanded a great deal of our attention.

The day was too sunny and warm to waste time sitting inside, so Rosa and I quickly got dressed and went out to enjoy the morning. We had recently given her a two-wheel bicycle for her fifth birthday, and it seemed like the perfect time for her to practise riding. I got the bike and some gardening tools out of the shed in the backyard and carried them out to the front of our house.

I stood on the front lawn watching Rosa wobble up and down the sidewalk. With one eye on her tiny helmeted head and one on the patch of soil before me, I started to dig away in our front garden beds, preparing the ground for planting a little later in the spring.

Rosa rolled by happily on her bike, turned proudly in the driveway, and went for another spin to the extent of her boundary, six houses away. She was content riding her bike for the remainder of the morning, and I was able to till and weed all of the garden beds. When I had finished my work, I sat on the top porch step and watched Rosa, who waved to me as she circled in the driveway yet again. It was such a beautiful day. The winter had been so harsh that this spring was especially appreciated.

I closed my eyes for a moment, enjoying the warmth of the sun on my face. Suddenly an image came into my mind of a middle-aged man sitting in a rocking chair and reading a newspaper on that very porch, although its floor was painted a bright red. From his clothing, and the chain leading to the watch in his vest pocket, the scene appeared to be set many, many decades ago.

I opened my eyes and gave my head a slight shake. That had been very peculiar; the vision had just seemed to spring into my mind. I closed my eyes again but experienced nothing unusual. Still, the image had been so vivid that I could clearly recall what the man looked like. The porch had appeared just the same, except that the floor boards were red instead of brown.

I took another look at Rosa riding up and down the street then left the porch for a moment to retrieve a small paring knife from the kitchen. When I came back out I looked around at the floor of the porch and decided to scrape in the far left corner. I kneeled down and began gently to peel away the many layers of paint affixed to the wide pine floor boards of the porch.

The first layer, of course, was brown. I gently lifted up a fleck of paint from the top coat and saw another layer of brown. The layer beneath that was also brown. Next, I came to a layer of blue. Beneath this, I found a layer of white, and finally, a layer of red. It was the last layer I found and had therefore been the first coat of paint applied. I stared at the colour for a moment and felt a slight chill. I had not known the porch had ever been painted red, yet the colour had been prominent in that flash of an image I had seen. The vision had been so clear, it was like sitting right next to the man reading the newspaper in his rocking chair.

Rosa noticed me crouched down on the porch.

"What is it, Mommy?" she asked as she drove up the walkway towards the stairs.

"I was just looking at this old floor," I said. "Do you want to ride for a few more minutes before we have to go in to get lunch ready?"

She nodded her head vigorously and went off for another spin. I sat down again on the top step, watching my daughter ride her new bicycle. I was having trouble forgetting the image of that man reading the newspaper. I had always been a history buff and enjoyed poring over books, photographs, and journals of other eras. I thought of all the historical events over the past century that would have made newspaper headlines to be read in a rocking chair on that very porch. It may have been a similarly warm spring day back in 1912, for instance, when the owner of that house sat on the porch reading about the sinking of the *Titanic*. But, I reminded myself, the house had actually been vacant for some reason then and would remain so for several more years. It would be a wonderful experience, though, to find a sample of some of the old newspapers that had been read there.

I finally sighed and called for Rosa to put her bicycle away as it was time for lunch. I had cleaned and redecorated every square inch of our house: if any previous owner had left any old newspapers behind I surely would have found them by now. Besides, I reasoned, the paper my mother had saved from the final day of World War II had been as carefully preserved as possible. I now had possession of that artifact, tucked safely away in a storage box, but it was so yellowed with age and brittle to the touch that it was almost impossible to handle it at all without the paper crumbling. If that one had so deteriorated, how could other old newspapers survive through the decades?

I had heard stories of homeowners discovering letters and newspapers behind walls and under floorboards, and I wished I could be that fortunate. Dismissing the notion of such a find as wishful thinking though, I led Rosa into the house and we began to prepare sandwiches for Kammie and Matt's lunch.

After the children had eaten and returned to school, Rosa and I spent the afternoon tidying up the house and doing some work on the back lawn. When Kammie and Matt arrived home again at four o'clock, we all went to the store to pick up some items I needed for dinner.

As we walked to the nearby market I explained to them that the garden areas were all ready to be planted now, and like last year, they could each have their own patch of soil in which to plant what they wished. That was exciting news for them as they enjoyed growing their own flowers and vegetables. Kammie had already decided that she wanted the area of garden right beside the front stairs, and as we approached the house on our way back, she pointed to the spot to lay her claim.

I was walking along with Kammie, discussing the best time to plant her flowers, and Matt and Rosa were following a few steps behind. As we approached the walkway to the porch, Kammie and I both stopped suddenly and stared at the front lawn. As we had walked towards the house, a newspaper had materialized right in front of our eyes. It had not been there one moment, but was definitely there the next. The paper was spread out, as though it was being read, on the front lawn beside the porch stairs.

Kammie and I looked at one another.

"Where on earth did that come from?" I finally managed to say.

"It must have got away from the paper boy when he was delivering his newspapers," Kammie suggested logically.

"Yes, it must have," I agreed. "But it seemed to appear out of nowhere. I didn't see it blowing down the street."

As I neared the paper to retrieve it, I saw that it was actually only one large piece of newsprint spread open, and therefore, four actual pages from a newspaper. The only thing that seemed unusual about it, at first, was its size. The paper was too wide and too short to be from our regular local newspaper. It looked new. I concluded that it could only have been outside for a short while, as it had rained the day before. When I picked up the paper to look at it, however, even before I noticed the advertisements and the photographs, I was surprised by the small size of the type. The numerous articles were much more compressed than those printed in any current newspaper.

"What is this?" I wondered aloud as I followed the children up the front steps to the porch.

When I finally looked at the top of the paper, I saw a name I did not recognize and a date I could scarcely believe: *The Mail and Empire*, Toronto, Thursday, August 17, 1933."

I almost dropped the newspaper in my shock. Kammie had seen the date by this time as well, and she looked at me with wide eyes and an open mouth.

"How can it be that old?" she asked. "It looks like it's brand new."

"I know," I said as my eyes scanned the paper, thinking it might be some kind of joke or novelty item.

The week before, a newspaper carrier had left several copies of a free weekly paper at the side of our house, apparently too tired to finish his route. The papers had sat between our house and our neighbour's for two days before they were discovered. In only that short period, they had turned yellowish and soggy from their exposure to the elements. I thought of those papers as I gently held this mint antique newspaper in my hands. Where could it have come from? How could it look and smell so new?

So many articles were crammed into the four pages of newsprint. There were stories about the many indigent citizens trying to survive the difficult times of what would come to be known as the Great Depression. But, the advertisements were fun to read: "Cruise the Great Lakes over the Week-end. From Toronto to Sault Ste. Marie. $15.00 Return." Another told the reader, "Today is Bargain Day at Eaton's: women's shoes–$1.89; all wool dresses–$2.95; real silk hosiery–.69; cotton pyjamas–$1.00; and Men's two-trousers all wool navy blue and plain gray serge suits–$20.00."

There were stories of tragedy as well: a little boy had drowned after becoming entangled in weeds in a river and a five-year-old had been scalded when he upset a kettle of boiling water. A lighter-toned feature, positioned at the bottom corner of the third page, was entitled "Home Run Standing." The baseball leaders were Foxx, Athletics, 35; Ruth, Yankees, 26; and Gehrig, Yankees, 20.

One of the most notable news story concerned the race riot at Christie Pits in Toronto, Ontario, the previous evening between the Jewish and non-Jewish spectators at a baseball game. Another article ran under the headline: "Germany Is Seen As World Menace ... Minister and Author Fears Result of Hitler Regime."

The children and I sat on the front porch, and I read them portions of news from the past. We all were amazed at finding this perfectly preserved piece of history and still puzzled at how it had come to be lying on our front lawn. I realized it had only been a few hours earlier that I had sat at that spot and wished for that very experience. Although I was thrilled with the page, I regretted it was not a complete copy.

"Where could this have come from?" I mused again.

"I know!" said Kammie. "I bet it came from under the porch!"

"No, it couldn't have," I said. "That's all closed in with brick and lattice. Not even a strong wind could have blown it out from under there. Besides, if it had been outside all these years, it wouldn't be in this kind of condition."

"Couldn't we just get a flashlight and check and see if there are more newspapers?" Kammie asked.

"Go ahead," I told her. She could get the flashlight from the kitchen if she wanted and see for herself, but I was sure that there was nothing under the porch.

Lattice covered the left side of the stairs, edging one of the garden beds that I had tilled and weeded that morning. Kammie kneeled down to look, and before she even turned on the flashlight, she let out a small gasp.

"What's that?" she said, pointing towards the lattice.

Matt, Rosa, and I hurried down the stairs to see what she had found. Just inside the lattice was what appeared to be a bundle of newspaper. I knew with certainty that there had been nothing there when I had done my gardening, and it was obvious from the embedded rusty nails in the lattice that it had not been disturbed in many years.

I sent Kammie in to fetch the hammer so I could remove the lattice and retrieve the item. As I waited for my daughter to come back with the tool I tried to estimate how old the paper could be. I knew no one had recently removed the lattice. When Ted had examined the underside of the porch the previous year to determine what would be needed to turn the porch into a sun room, he had shone his light through the holes of the lattice, but he had not removed the wood itself. Nor had he mentioned seeing a newspaper under there. I peered at what was obviously a complete edition and not just one large sheet of newsprint.

Kammie gave me the hammer, and I carefully began to pry the nails out of the wooden lattice so I could remove it. The nails were so thoroughly rusted in place that it was some time before I could finally pull the lattice from the side of the stairs.

When I had retrieved the folded newspaper, the children gathered around me to see its date. It was obviously not a copy of our small local paper; it was much too thick for that. We were all astonished when we read: "*The Toronto Daily Star*, Wednesday, November 28, 1934." I later learned that this name had been shortened to *The Toronto Star* in 1971.

It was beyond my comprehension how two Toronto newspapers, one complete and one partial and long defunct, printed within fifteen months of each other in the 1930s and in excellent condition, had come to be there only hours after I had been hoping for such a find. Both old newspapers had appeared out of nowhere, just as I had wished after seeing the image of the man reading a paper on the front porch. It seemed unbelievable.

I took the paper up onto the porch and spread it out on the floor. We gathered around the old newspaper, and I looked through its pages, sharing the various news stories I saw with the children. The main story of the day was about "Baby Face" Nelson, the lead member of the late John Dillinger's gang, who, along with two FBI agents, had been killed in a shoot-out the previous night. Another page informed us that the Dionne Quintuplets had just celebrated their sixth-month birthday and were now expected to live an average life span. Still another story concerned silent film star Douglas Fairbanks, who had been cited as a co-respondent in Lady Ashley's divorce case against Lord Ashley and therefore had been ruled by the court to pay all the costs involved.

The page that delighted the children the most featured the comic strips of the day. They smiled and giggled at the antics of Popeye, Li'l Abner, and Tarzan and the Lion Man. The entertainment page encouraged the public, for the admission price of twenty-five cents, to see such films as *Anne of Green Gables*, starring Anne Shirley; *The Girl from Missouri*, with Jean Harlow, and *The Merry Widow*, with Jeanette McDonald.

This remarkable piece of history also featured articles that contained first-hand accounts of the often insurmountable hardship the Great Depression was casting on the nation. Unlike history books, those articles presented the human side of that era.

I was eager for Ted to get home at dinner time so I could show him our amazing finds. As I refolded the newspaper, Kammie touched my hand, and I looked into her worried eyes.

"We aren't going to bring that into the house, are we?" she asked me quietly.

"Of course we are," I said, still excited.

"I think we should put it back," Kammie insisted.

I then understood why she was worried. As with the old cream jar, ink-well, and button found in the backyard, bringing this paper into the house could cause an increase in our disturbances. Although we still experienced occasional paranormal activity, the frequency and intensity had lessened after we had replaced those items in the ground. As that was not a risk I was prepared to take, with some disappointment I put the old newspaper, from November 28, 1934, back under the porch, exactly where we had found it. The page from the August 17, 1933 paper, however, had not been contained within the property but had been found lying on the front lawn. I thought it would therefore be safe to take it in the house, and I carefully folded it up and carried it up to my desk in the attic.

When Ted got home later that evening we told him what we had found. He of course found it a little hard to believe, but after I had shown him the page from the 1933 edition of *The Mail and Empire*, he could not logically explain how it had materialized. He too was shocked that a paper that old could appear to be that freshly printed.

"Where did you say you found the other paper?" Ted asked.

"Under the porch," Kammie told him.

"I didn't see any newspapers, and I spent a lot of time looking under there," he said.

"I know," she giggled, amused at her father's bewilderment.

"It was leaning against the inside of the lattice, right where we've replaced it," I said.

Ted went outside to see that for himself. I assumed his main concern was whether I had damaged the lattice, but he came back into the house shaking his head.

"Who could have put that there, and when?" he asked.

"I don't know. But you have a logical explanation for it, right?" I smiled at my husband.

He had to admit, that time, he definitely did not.

Inkwell, button, and cream jar: found buried in the backyard while the additional room was being constructed. As directed by psychic, we replaced these objects back into the ground in an attempt to halt the increased paranormal activity.

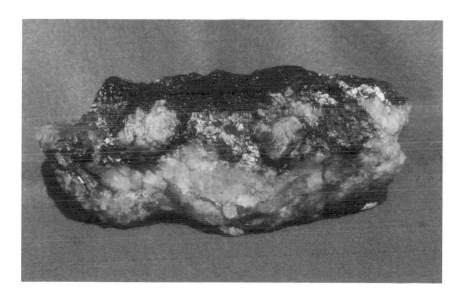

Large piece of quartz containing Fool's Gold found buried in the backyard, which was also eventually replaced.

135

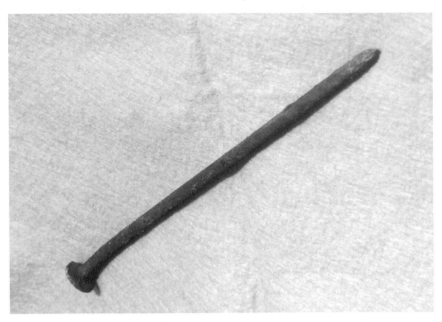

Large rusty nail that seemed to drop out of thin air.

Mail and Empire Toronto newspaper from August 17, 1933 which suddenly appeared spread open to page five on our front lawn. It was in perfect condition when originally found, but by the time the photograph was taken three months later it was starting to show signs of yellowing due to its actual age.

The Toronto Daily Star from November 28, 1934 which appeared behind the lattice on the front porch. The newspaper was in pristine condition when it was first discovered. When the photograph was taken three months later rampant deterioration had already taken place.

15

PAGE FIVE

One Sunday evening, later that spring, I found myself unable to settle in the family room with the others as I impatiently waited for a phone call from Beverly. She had attended a family wedding with her sister, Dennise, that weekend and had told me she would call when she got home. Finally, late in the evening, the telephone rang. Beverly told me that Dennise had been intrigued by what she had told her.

As Dennise was unable to visit our town, and therefore, our home anytime soon, I had described the paranormal events we had experienced to Beverly, who had then shared that information with Dennise. Even if she was unable to visit the house herself, I hoped that she could offer some advice on the matter based on what she heard.

Although the sightings of the actual spirits had frightened me the most, I found the appearance of the nail and the two newspapers to be the most bizarre and inexplicable incidents. I had asked Beverly if she could question Dennise about those events in particular. Was it at all possible that those materialized items had been meant as a gift or a sign? And, if so, what did they mean?

Dennise had told Beverly that she had spirit guides that communicated with her, and it was through those guides that she had received information about our situation. When asked about the newspapers, she had said that those definitely had been given to us by the spirits and that there was an important reason for their appearance. She had been told that the answer to their significance for us was on page five of the newspapers.

Beverly apologized for that scant bit of information. She explained that she had not had a lot of time to speak to her sister privately and did not feel comfortable talking about that sort of thing in a crowd. I was grateful to receive any help and thanked my friend for her trouble.

Unable to wait until morning to satisfy my piqued curiosity, I went up to the attic to retrieve the old page of newsprint and spread it out as it had been when we had found it on the front lawn. I looked at the number at the top of the right-hand page and felt my heart begin to race. It was page five.

I began a thorough search through all the page's articles and advertisements, but searching for something significant was like looking for a needle in a haystack. Any one of the news stories could contain a message, including the top centred article entitled "Two Brilliant Students," which featured a photograph of a young man and woman and listed all their academic accomplishments. Feeling discouraged, I folded the old paper and put it back on the desk.

During that summer, my friend, Sylvia, planned to visit. I had been keeping her informed about the strange happenings in our household, and she was anxious to see evidence of paranormal activity while she stayed with us. She seemed more fascinated than frightened by all my tales of the haunting.

When her car pulled up, the children and I went out to greet her, leaving the house empty behind us. As I helped Sylvia unload her suitcase and bags from the trunk, I noticed that Kammie was staring at the foyer window. I tried to get her attention as I handed over a bag for her to carry in for us, but she stood transfixed, seemingly unaware of anything else.

"What's wrong?" I asked, seeing Kammie's disturbed expression.

"Who's that?" she whispered to me, not wanting Sylvia to overhear.

"Who's who?" I asked, looking at the empty foyer window.

"She was just there," Kammie said.

I glanced over at Sylvia, hoping she had not been able to hear our conversation. I did not want her to be afraid to enter the house from the moment of her arrival. Sylvia, though, was engaged in lively chatter with Rosa and Matt about their summer activities.

"I don't see anyone," I told Kammie.

"Someone was looking out of the window and then went up the stairs," my daughter said.

"What did they look like?" I asked quietly.

"I'm pretty sure it was a lady. She was dark, and I couldn't really tell what she was wearing. She was watching us. Then I saw her move away from the window, and it looked like she went up the stairs."

Kammie continued to stare at the window for a moment, then shrugged her shoulders and took the bag from my hand. She did not seem concerned about what she had seen and soon joined the other children in telling Sylvia all about her summer holiday plans.

The first thing Sylvia wanted to look at, once the children had gone back outside to play, was the newspaper we had found on the front lawn. As I chose to not overwhelm her with too much information, I did not tell her what Kammie had just seen in the foyer, but did take her up to the attic to see the page of newsprint. We spread the paper out on the floor and, paying particular attention to page five, closely examined its contents. I explained to her that when we had first found the paper, it had not smelled like old newsprint. Although now, a few months later, it did have a slight odour and was beginning to yellow, it still did not appear to be nearly as old as it actually was.

The article about Germany was the first thing to catch Sylvia's eye, and I agreed it did seem the most newsworthy. However, I did not understand what the significance could be of a news article that warned of an impending world war.

"What's on page five of the paper under the porch?" Sylvia asked.

"I don't know. I can't remember. We only looked at it that one time and then put it back," I said.

We looked at each other and then raced down the flights of stairs to the porch to retrieve the old paper from behind the lattice. Ted, arriving home from work, volunteered to pry the wood loose for us, more out of concern that the fragile piece might be broken if done incorrectly than out of interest in our quest for clues.

As my husband handed the bundle up to me, I stared at it in confusion.

"This isn't the same paper," I said.

"Yes, it is," Ted assured me. "It was exactly where you left it."

"But look at it!" I said. "It didn't look anything like this when we found it three months ago."

The newspaper now appeared to be every bit as old as its date indicated. The pages were so yellowed and brittle with decay that it was scarcely possible to make out the print at all. As I handled it, large pieces broke off and crumbled. I didn't understand how it could have deteriorated to that extent.

I gingerly carried the remains of the newspaper up onto the porch and opened it up to see if anything could still be read on the fifth page. Most of the paper was now illegible and some pieces were missing altogether, but, amazingly, there was an article at the top centre of page five, in the same location as the other newspaper's fifth-page story. That article, too, warned about the very real probability of war. Its headline read: "Preparation For War Proceeds In Germany." It informed the reader that Hitler was telling the German people that the rest of the world hated them and wanted to destroy them, but he would lead them to victory over that oppression.

That article had been written fifteen months after the story in *The Mail and Empire*, yet they both spoke of the threat of a world war, and they both appeared in the same location on page five. Perhaps the most extraordinary fact was that the *Toronto Daily Star* article was nearly the only legible story left on the page.

Sylvia read the article again.

"This must be the message," she said.

After she spoke those words, the three of us saw, through the open front door, the light in the foyer turn on.

"Is this the message?" Sylvia asked, staring wide-eyed into the foyer and then turning to me with a nervous smile.

The light turned off and then on, twice. At first I felt a sense of relief that someone else, besides me and the children, had seen that happening. I looked at Ted to see if he too had seen the flickering light and realized from the look on his face that he had. But, it was disturbing that the message could possibly be related to the approach of a world war. The three of us looked at one another soberly for a moment.

"Where are the kids?" Ted asked, thinking that perhaps one of them might have been inside playing with the switch.

"All three are playing basketball at the side of the house," I said, which he quickly confirmed with a glance around the corner.

Ted just smiled and shook his head, again refusing to believe there was not a reasonable explanation for what we had just seen. I was growing frustrated with his refusal to admit something unusual was happening in our home and to take it seriously.

"What will it take to convince you?" I asked him in exasperation. "I wish something else would happen, specifically to you, that would prove to you that this is real."

My husband smiled at my frustration. Ted would admit that he had heard the footsteps many times and of course the smoke detector alarms woke him up as well at night. He acknowledged that it was strange that Piper refused to go upstairs to the second floor, and he knew the children all claimed to have seen spirits in the house. But he still refused to admit that anything supernatural was at the root of all of this.

Sylvia, now a firm believer after being in the house only a few hours, laughed at my husband's stubbornness.

"I think you're too scared to admit this is actually happening," she teased him.

"No way!" he laughed, heading back into the house. "Who wants a beer?"

Ted went into the kitchen to get us drinks, and Sylvia and I continued to look through the legible sections of the old newspaper. I decided to get my camera and take a picture of it as a keepsake before it completely decomposed. I also went up and got the sheet of newsprint from the attic. Although it was still in good condition, having been kept inside, on my desk, I knew it might be only a matter of time before it deteriorated too. I brought it outside and spread it out onto the lawn, as it had been the day we found it, and took a picture of it as well. Even if I was not able to figure out the significance of page five and the paper did decompose, at least I would have a photograph as a permanent reminder of finding it.

When Ted came out with our bottles of beer, he helped me to replace the old newspaper under the porch, and I took the other piece of newsprint back up to the attic. We then all sat in the living room and relaxed. Ted took a few sips from his beer, and then left it on the coffee table to answer the phone in the kitchen. When he came back, he lifted the bottle towards his mouth for another drink. As he did so, the beer suddenly erupted into his face like a small volcano. It shocked him so much, he almost dropped the bottle. Sylvia and I both jumped up from where we were sitting to help Ted clean up. His face was covered in beer, and it was dripping from his clothes and hair.

"Did you shake that up?" he asked me, thinking it had been some kind of practical joke.

"No! We didn't touch it," I insisted, and Sylvia quickly agreed.

None of us had ever seen a bottle of beer erupt like that before, and after the initial shock, we all broke into peels of laughter. It had made quite a mess but the look on Ted's face had been something to see. We started to laugh all over again every time we thought of it.

"Do you think maybe it happened specifically to you to convince you this is real?" I asked my husband jokingly, reminding him of what I had said on the porch. He laughed as he towel-dried his wet hair and warned me that I should be careful about what I wished for from then on.

"Let's try that again," Ted said, and got another bottle out of the refrigerator. He took off the cap and let the beer stand still for a few minutes before he attempted to take a drink. Nothing happened. He took several more sips and still nothing unusual occurred. Finally, after convincing himself that the last beer's eruption had just been a fluke, he settled down comfortably on the couch and took another drink. That time the beer again shot straight into his face, but with even more force than before. No one laughed then, though. It was much too strange to be humorous, although Ted's look of stark horror gave me a bit of satisfaction. Even he could not logically explain away this phenomenon.

From that day on, Ted was unable to enjoy a bottle of beer in his own home. If he were drinking a bottle anywhere else, nothing unusual would occur. But if he attempted to drink a beer in the house or anywhere on our property, he could be assured it would shoot right into his face. It would not erupt when the cap was removed, or when he might expect it to, but only when his guard was down. Neither of us really drank much, but in our amazement with this oddity, we tested it on many occasions. We tried switching bottles, but it still erupted in Ted's face. He even tried drinking the beer from a glass, but it shot up as it was being poured into the stein. It eventually became quite a family joke, and even the children would gather around to watch what happened when Daddy tried to drink a beer. But, although it exasperated Ted, he refused to acknowledge there was anything unusual behind it.

Finally, after months of that activity, I had the satisfaction of hearing my husband admit that it really was strange and something must have been going on that could not be explained or denied. And that was all it took. There was never another eruption. After that admission, he was allowed to drink his beer in peace.

16

A GIFT OF FLOWERS

Early one morning after Ted had walked sleepily into the bath-room, I heard him anxiously call for me. I went in to see what was wrong and looked in the direction of his gaze. A cabinet stood in front of a mirror that covered a large portion of one of the bathroom walls. On top of the counter was a huge, decorative oil lamp. Together Ted and I stared at two tiny hand prints pressed firmly and clearly onto the mirror directly behind the glass chimney of the lamp.

The hand prints were positioned beyond the reach of any our children, and it would have been impossible to have left those marks without removing the oil lamp. Yet it looked as if a very young child had been staring at their reflection and then placed two little hands on either side of the face's image.

Upon examining the impression of the hands, the most inexplicable feature about them was their size. Rosa was the smallest member of our household. Yet when we compared her hands to those ones, hers were twice as large. The prints obviously had been made by a child of perhaps only one or two years of age. I was not frightened, but very bewildered, by their appearance.

Our children were just as amazed by them. Ted seemed much more disturbed by those hand prints than anything else we had experienced, and I watched him inspect them with obvious concern. That was definitely something he could not rationalize away. The prints were distinctly apparent on the glass; we all clearly saw them, and they could not be dismissed as a figment of anyone's imagination.

I wiped the prints off of the mirror, but they reappeared three more times in different locations. Finally, I was able to clean them off for good.

We spent the next day preparing for a two-week holiday on the coast. The children were out of school for the summer and everyone was looking forward to our vacation. As I was packing up groceries from the kitchen to take with us, I heard Piper begin to whine at the back door. I walked through the family room to let her out into the yard and glanced out the window as I passed by. To my astonishment, I saw the full blooms of a rose bush just below the window sill.

I had decided to reclaim the neglected small garden in which Kammie had found her large sample of pyrite, now located next to the new family room, after all the debris from the construction of the new addition had been cleared. I had dug in the area for most of one afternoon, and after hitting a piece of rock sticking up out of the grass, I had unearthed what turned out to be all the original pieces of stone that had once surrounded the garden. After I had hosed down the dirt-caked pieces of stone, I replaced them, like a jigsaw puzzle, where they had once been positioned. When I had finished, the garden had been completely restored to its original condition, except, of course, for its flowers. I had planted some impatiens that bloomed there nicely, adding bright colour to the backyard.

That spring, however, I had noticed a plant growing up through the soil and I had wondered what it was. I thought it was the result of another buried walnut, forgotten by a squirrel. Mr. Ryan, the former owner, had been an avid gardener and most of the perennials and bushes on our property were the result of his green thumb. Still, I had only planted impatiens, and prior to that, the garden had been covered with grass.

This mystery plant had obviously been a rose bush, which was now bearing dozens of buds in various stages of growth. It was incredible that the small, barely noticeable plant had become an incredible flowering shrub in such a short period of time. It had grown as fast as the walnut tree, and the colour and fragrance of the roses were spectacular.

When Kammie came into the yard she mentioned that the flowers' smelled the same as an aroma she had noticed in the house on several occasions when we had first moved in. She had often asked if anyone else could smell roses, especially on the second floor, but no one seemed to detect it but her.

I knew that when our two-week holiday was over the roses would no longer be in bloom, so I decided to cut some off and hang them upside down in the house, to dry. They were such an unexpected treat and so beautiful that I wanted to save the blossoms and use them to decorate our home. I snipped away with a pair of kitchen scissors and piled the stems into a basket. There were even more buds on the rose-laden branches than I had seen from the window above.

As I pruned the bush, I heard a tap on Donelle's kitchen window, and I turned to see our neighbour watching me as she talked away to someone on the telephone. I smiled and waved at the elderly lady and went back into the house to hang up the roses for drying. Later that afternoon, as I sat on the front porch and waited for Ted to get home so we could leave for the cottage, Donelle walked out her front door.

"Where did that rose bush come from?" she called over.

"I really don't know. It's beautiful though, isn't it?"

"Didn't you plant it?" the old woman asked.

I shrugged my shoulders and shook my head.

"I was on the phone with Mr. Ryan when I saw you clipping off the blooms. I told him you had some beautiful roses growing under that window, and he said you must have planted that rose bush when you moved in because he had grown nothing there."

"I never planted it," I said.

"Well, who did?" my neighbour asked.

"I have no idea. I just noticed it this spring, but I didn't plant it."

"I'm surprised at how big it is. I just noticed it for the first time today, and I don't know how I could have missed seeing it. I'm always looking at your yard through my kitchen window," Donelle went on.

"I just noticed myself that it had grown that tall and had all those roses on it," I told her, although I realized it must have sounded impossible for me to have missed seeing a rose bush like that growing right outside my own back door.

When Ted got home I showed him the multitude of roses I had clipped off the bush. He was as surprised as everyone else that the beautiful plant had sprouted up out of nowhere. We left then for the cottage and did not give the rose bush much thought while on our holiday.

Upon our return two weeks later, I asked Matt to put the dog into the yard after the long car ride. When he and Piper had reached the family room, I heard him call for me.

A Gift of Flowers

"What is it?" I asked him from the foyer where I had dropped some of our bags from the car.

"Come and see all the flowers!" he said.

I walked into the family room and joined Matt at the window. The rose bush was once again covered in buds, at least as many as I had pruned before we left. It was a gorgeous sight. Where the bush had come from and how it was able to produce so many lovely roses in such a short amount of time was a mystery to us, but it was a beautiful addition to our garden.

I tried to answer the many questions I had about the bush by researching roses on the Internet, but could not find the information I needed. I finally sent an e-mail message to one of the gardening sites, explaining how quickly the rose bush had grown and how it produced dozens of roses. I wanted to know how it was possible. I never received a response from the gardening site expert, who probably thought I had been joking. I came to accept and enjoy the roses as they were and put aside my questions.

Several days later Beverly called. She told me she had been talking with Dennise the night before. They had discussed our home and Dennise had repeated the information she had received regarding a message located on page five in the newspapers.

"She also asked how you liked your gift of flowers," Beverly said.

"What?" I asked, surprised by the question.

"Dennise said that she had been told that the spirits had given you a gift of flowers, and she wondered how you liked them. I told her I didn't understand what she meant, but she said that you would know. Do you?"

Dennise could not have known about the rose bush as I had not mentioned it to Beverly. Yet thanks to her message, I now understood that the roses were meant as a wonderful gift, and the bush became even more special to me.

151

"Yes, I love the flowers," I said. I could only shake my head in bewilderment as I stared out the window into the garden.

The bush bloomed repeatedly throughout the summer, and I continued to clip the rose-covered stems. I was running out of places to hang the flowers to dry but did not want to see them wither after they had bloomed. The dried rose wreaths soon adorned every room, and their presence seemed to add a peacefulness to our home.

The winter that followed was very severe, and more than half a metre of snow covered the ground by late December. On Christmas Day we happened to look out at the bush. Although most of it was buried in a drift, one branch poked out of the snow bearing a freshly bloomed rose. We thought it was a remarkable Christmas gift.

A few weeks later, Ted and I were out shovelling snow from our front walkway. While Matt was at a friend's house, Kammie was curled up on the love seat and Rosa sat on the floor beside the fireplace as they watched a movie together in the living room. A very heavy wood-framed mirror hung directly above the fireplace mantle, and I had loosely arrayed dried rose blossoms along the top of its frame. The mantle was decorated with family portraits in brass, wood, and ceramic frames and a large, fragile antique oil lamp.

While the girls were watching the movie, the nail came out from the picture hook on which the mirror had been suspended by a wire. When the mirror fell, landing a foot below on the mantle, it dislodged none of the fragile items around it, and it remained angled at the same thirty degrees from the wall at which it had been suspended on the wire.

If the force of the fall had not been enough to propel the mirror and most of the other fragile items off of the mantle to the floor below, then surely gravity should have caused the mirror to topple forward. And if that had occurred, Rosa, who was sitting directly beneath the mantle, would have been seriously hurt. The spray of shattered glass from the broken mirror, picture frames and the oil lamp would have harmed both of the girls.

Yet the mirror remained frozen at that impossible thirty degree angle on the mantle and not a single petal of the dried rose blossoms atop its wooden frame had stirred when Ted and I came into the house a few minutes later. The girls met us at the door and excitedly told us what had happened. When I understood what they were saying and looked into the living room to see the huge mirror on the mantle, I raced over, thinking it was about to fall. It remained suspended until I reached my hands up to grab it. Then, as I was about to touch it, all of the dried rose blossoms fell from the top of its frame and it started to fall forward. I caught its sides in my hands, but Ted had to lift its heavy weight down from the mantle.

He leaned the mirror against the wall and inspected it while I gathered up the rose petals scattered all over the mantle and floor and listened to the girls talk about what had happened when the mirror had fallen.

"I don't know how the things on the fireplace didn't get knocked over when the mirror fell, especially that big lamp," Kammie said, and Rosa nodded in agreement.

"I thought that mirror was going to fall on my head!" Rosa said. "But it just stayed there until you came in."

Ted immediately installed a new and more secure picture hook into the wall above the mantle and was readying to hang the mirror once again over the fireplace. I asked him to wait until I had given it a good dusting. I figured that would be a good time to clean the hard to reach mirror, and went into the kitchen to get the glass cleaner and a cloth. Just as I was about to begin spraying the glass,

I noticed some marks near the top of the mirror. Two tiny hand prints, the same size as the little ones we had seen on the bathroom mirror, could be seen. I wondered if I was only imagining them due to the stress I felt over my daughters' close call, but Ted and the girls could also see them.

Kammie and Rosa told me that it had looked as if someone were holding the mirror in place after it fell from the wall. With what appeared to be a toddler's hand prints on the glass of the mirror, I wondered if that had been exactly what occurred. I shuddered to think of what might have happened to my girls. If someone's hands had left those marks when holding back the mirror, I was very grateful for the intervention.

17

ANGELS IN THE DOORWAY

Matt's room was no longer the centre of any unusual activity. It had been some time since he had mentioned seeing or hearing anything at all out of the ordinary, and he had been able to sleep undisturbed. One night, however, he woke me when he called out in a loud, anxious voice.

When I hurried into his bedroom, I found him sitting up in bed with a worried expression on his face.

"What's wrong?" I asked.

"There was a boy in my room," he said.

"What did he look like?" I asked, as I sat down on his bed. I wondered if it had been the same young blond boy I had seen some time ago, running down the stairs.

"He was bigger than me. He was maybe about twelve," my son estimated.

"What was he doing?" I asked.

"He was just standing right there." He pointed to a spot beside his bed, near the door leading up to the attic. "He was standing there watching me," he added.

"What did he look like?" I asked again.

"He was sad," Matt said quietly. "His clothes were like rags and really dirty, like he was poor or something. And his head looked funny."

"What do you mean?" I asked.

"I don't know," he struggled to explain. "It was a funny shape, like it had been hurt. His hair was really short, even shorter than Daddy's. I think it was blond, but it looked all muddy and dirty, like his clothes. And his skin was a funny colour, kind of blue and gray. He looked at me like he was so sad. Why would he be so sad?"

"I don't know, honey," I said as I held him close to me.

Matt seemed more concerned about the reason for the boy's unhappiness than frightened or upset by the sighting.

"I'm okay, Mommy," he assured me as he lay back down under his covers and prepared to go to sleep.

"Do you want to sleep in our room tonight?" I offered.

"No, it's all right," he said.

I kissed my son goodnight and went back to our bedroom. I lay awake thinking about what Matt had seen and the possible reasons that the haunting was still occurring. We had put back everything from the backyard that had been found there. What else could we have done to stop that activity in our home?

It was dawn when I suddenly had a thought. I got up and went into Kammie's room, but I could not see the object. Before I returned to my bed, I went to check on Matt to see if he were sleep-

156

ing soundly. When I walked into his room, I saw what I had been seeking. Displayed on his dresser, not far from the attic door, was the large piece of pyrite Kammie had found in the backyard. We had placed all the items we had found back into the ground except that one. Because he enjoyed looking at the quartz and gold-coloured minerals, Kammie had allowed Matt to keep the sample overnight in his room.

I wondered if there could be a connection between the sad-looking boy in the ragged clothes and the piece of pyrite. Perhaps he had been brought to that area by his father, who had been lured by the promise of gold that proved to be worthless. Could the boy have felt some connection to the piece of Fool's Gold similar to the young girl's seeming attachment to the ink-well, jar, and button?

That morning, as Ted and the children ate their breakfast, I carried the heavy piece of pyrite outside and laid it on top of the buried items beneath the family room addition. It would serve as a marker for those articles, but it was also very near to where it had been discovered. Kammie had agreed when I explained we had to return it too. Now everything was back in its proper place, and I hoped that would give the spirits and our family some peace.

Soon after Matt had seen the sad boy in his bedroom, Rosa began to talk about angels. I thought she might have overheard a discussion about what her brother had seen, and I was concerned that it may have frightened her. Some subtle questioning, however, revealed that Rosa had no idea that Matt had seen a spirit by his bed, nor did she seem afraid at all of the thought that angels, as she called them, were in our home. After seeing the hand prints on the bathroom and living room mirrors, she seemed to accept their reality all the more.

"I know what angels look like!" she exclaimed with great excitement to me one morning.

I smiled at her, but felt slightly uneasy.

"How do you know that Rosa?" I asked her.

"Because I saw two angels in my room last night!" she announced happily.

"Where were they?" I questioned.

"They were standing in the doorway waving to me!" she said.

"Oh, my," I said and forced a smile. "And what did they look like?"

"One was a little boy and the other one was a bigger girl," Rosa replied. "I think they were brother and sister because they looked like each other and both of them had the same kind of yellow hair."

"Did they talk to you?" I asked.

"Nope. They just stood there and waved to me, and then they were gone. But I really did see them, and I know they were angels."

"I think they were too. Did it surprise you to see them standing there?" I asked softly as I brushed her hair back from her eyes.

"Kind of," Rosa said. "I was laying in my bed and looked out the door into the hall because I thought Matt and Kammie were coming to see me. When I saw who was standing there, I knew it wasn't them."

"Have you ever seen them before?" I asked.

"Nope. Just last night. But it was like they knew me, like they were my friends. They waved to me as if they really liked me," she smiled at the memory.

"Well, who wouldn't like a nice little girl like you?" I said as I cuddled her up in my arms. Rosa squealed with laughter and tried to wriggle out of my embrace.

She had not mentioned seeing the girl who waved to her from her bedroom window for a long time, but I knew she would remember her. Those two spirits must have been different entities or she would have recognized the girl and said so.

I thought of the times over the past few weeks when Rosa had insisted she had heard a little boy calling for his mother. She had entered kindergarten the previous autumn but was only in school during the mornings. In the afternoon, on several occasions, Rosa had asked me, "Didn't you hear him call 'Mommy!'? It was really loud. Like when Matt calls you if something is wrong and he needs you to help him."

I did not hear the voice, and would explain that to Rosa. It did remind me though of the one time both Rosa and I had heard a child calling for his mother when Matt and Kammie had been home for lunch, and we had mistakenly thought it was Matt calling for me. Shortly after that, I had seen the little boy in gray running through the foyer.

After hearing Rosa's description of the children who appeared at her door the previous night, I wondered if it was the same boy I had seen that day and the girl both Kammie and I had sighted on separate occasions. Perhaps it was the same little boy whom Rosa repeatedly heard calling for his mother. At that thought, I felt an overwhelming sense of sadness that any child should be lost from their parent.

Several days later Rosa called me into her bedroom to tell me she had heard a girl singing. She asked me if Kammie had come home early from school. I told her the children were not due home for another hour yet. I thought her hearing someone singing was only wishful thinking on her part. I knew how much she missed her brother and sister when they were not home to play with her.

As we were leaving her room to head downstairs, I noticed one of Rosa's dresser drawers was opened. I sent her back to close it before she joined me. As I started down the stairway, Rosa called to me again. I went back up and found her standing in her doorway, pointing to the dresser.

"Mommy!" she gasped. "It closed by itself!"

I looked to where she was pointing and saw that the dresser drawer was now closed tightly. It took me a moment to realize, though, that Rosa had not had enough time to go back into her room, close the drawer, and run to the doorway to call me in the second or two that had elapsed.

I stared at the dresser in disbelief. Apparently it had closed by itself, and I was just as surprised as my daughter.

"Did you see it close?" I asked Rosa.

"No, but I heard it when I got to the door," my little girl said.

The two of us stood in the doorway for another moment, staring at the dresser.

"I think that angel did it for me," Rosa finally said.

"What angel?" I asked.

"The one I heard singing before, remember? I thought it was Kammie, but I guess it was an angel," she said calmly.

I nodded at her and looked again at the dresser. The musical ballerina figurine that stood atop it suddenly turned on, and "The Nutcracker Suite" filled the room as the china dancer spun around and around in time with the music.

Rosa gasped audibly but seemed more delighted than scared by those bizarre events. Whereas Matt had been frightened by his first encounters with the spirits, Rosa appeared to feel fortunate to be having such extraordinary experiences. She seemed to accept the existence of the "angels" as a simple fact of life, and it never occurred to her that there was anything to fear from them.

18

POWER PROBLEMS

It was a very hot day near the end of summer, and the children and I were eating lunch in the family room. The stereo was on in one corner, while a fan cooled the air in the room. When I heard a knock at the front door, I left the children eating and went to answer it.

I opened the door to the electrical inspector, who introduced himself and explained the reason for his visit. Although the new room had been completed for quite some time, he had not yet inspected the site to check on the wiring's safety.

Knowing that the electrical service in the new room worked perfectly well, I expected it to take only minutes for him to see that everything was fine. I took him directly to the basement so that he could see the new electrical panel box. Everything seemed to be in order, and we went up to the family room so he could check the outlets. Since it was such a sunny day, no lights had been turned on, but I realized when we entered the room that both the fan and the stereo had stopped working.

"Who turned those off?" I asked the children.

"No one," Kammie explained. "As soon as you went to get the door the fan and stereo just stopped working."

I looked over at the inspector, but I did not know what to say. He could see the vacuum cleaner that I had used just that morning standing in the corner. It was obvious the fan had been on, as it was too hot to sit in a room with southern exposure on such a sunny day and not be uncomfortable without circulating the air. The power obviously had been working properly just prior to his inspection, but it now was off. He examined the various outlets in the room and went back downstairs to check the panel box again. No fuse had blown and everything on the panel box was in perfect order. No other room in the house was affected, and the man was completely baffled.

"I've been doing this job a long time," he told me, "but I've never seen anything like this. I really can't tell what's causing this problem."

I immediately thought of the times in the past when the stereo had turned on by itself but could not bring myself to admit those incidents to a stranger. I hoped the inspector would find a logical, scientific reason as to why the room suddenly had no power.

"Bill Watson was the electrician?" he confirmed with me.

"That's right. He updated the electrical service for the entire house when he did the new wiring."

"You better get in touch with him and explain that you have a problem here. I'll be back after he's has taken care of it."

I called the electrician and told him what had happened. When he came to our house later that afternoon, he was as bewildered as the inspector had been. He could find no reason for the loss of power, and nothing he did seemed to help. While the electrician was there trying to fix the problem, I quickly took the children shopping for a new light fixture for the foyer that I wanted him to install. Perhaps it was only an electrical problem that caused it to turn on and off by itself.

When we returned home, the electrician was packing up his tools. I could hear music from the stereo playing in the family room and knew the electricity had been restored.

"What was wrong with it?" I asked.

"I still don't know," he answered truthfully. "I went out to the truck to get something, and when I came back in, everything seemed to be working fine. I never did anything, and I still can't figure out what the problem was."

I thought I knew what might have caused the power outage but said nothing. I showed Bill the new Victorian-style fixture for the foyer and asked if he could install it in place of the old one before he left. I was pleased with how it looked when he was done.

"The old one always turned on and off," Rosa told the electrician.

He smiled at my little girl, not understanding what she meant. "You won't have any problems with this one," he assured her.

When Ted got home from work I told him about the electrical problem we had experienced in the family room earlier that day. He walked around the room and checked the light switches and outlets, but everything was now working properly.

The inspector came back the following afternoon, and as I walked towards the front door to let him in, I quietly asked whomever was listening not to fool around with the electricity again. The inspector was pleased to see that the power had been restored, and he quickly completed his inspection.

To my relief, the new light in the foyer did seem to work much better. It remained on when it was turned on, and off when it was turned off. In fact, for a while after that, everything seemed normal again in our home.

On November 11, Remembrance Day, Rosa and I were walking past a shop downtown where a display had been set up to commemorate the local soldiers who had fought in World Wars I and II. As we stopped to look at the old photographs and news clippings, a name from the list of soldiers killed in action caught my eye. It was that of William Neen, the soldier who had rented our house in 1917 from the Barkers. He had died in World War I, just as I had thought when I had researched the house and found no further record of him.

That night, after the children were in bed, Ted and I watched a television program about Flanders Field. I told Ted about William Neen and explained that he had been killed in action overseas during the war. As I did so, the new light in the foyer went out. We looked at one another, exasperated at having gone to the expense of replacing the fixture only to have the same problem. When I went into the foyer to look at the fixture, however, I realized that only three of the four light bulbs had gone out and apparently needed replacing.

The next day, after purchasing new light bulbs, I went to the basement and got the ladder I would need to reach the foyer light. When I looked at the bulbs still in the fixture, it was no longer possible to tell which had burned out. When I had inspected the light the previous night, and even that morning, I could clearly see three that were blackened. When I had returned home from the store, just moments earlier, the fixture had still had only one working bulb. But now, as I stood on the ladder examining the light, all four bulbs appeared to be fine. I got down off of the ladder and turned the hall light switch on to confirm which bulbs needed replacing. All four of the bulbs lit up, and it was no longer necessary to replace any of them.

That became the new pattern of the foyer light. It would not turn on and off completely as it had with the old fixture, but periodically, one, two, three, or all four bulbs would appear to burn out and would remain that way until an attempt was made to replace them. Then, as soon as the ladder was brought up from the basement in readiness to restore the light's brightness, all four bulbs would begin to work flawlessly once more.

The telephone also began to cause us some frustration. At first we thought we were the random target of a prank caller and gave little attention to the frequent and annoying hang-ups we received. When the phone calls disturbed us up to twenty times a day, for days at a time, it eventually became a real nuisance. They would stop for a while, only to begin again with equal persistence. We bought a new telephone that featured caller identification, but that did not solve the problem. Whomever was dialing us registered as "unknown caller," and when we picked up the receiver, no one was ever there.

It took a while for me to wonder whether there was a connection between the problem with the telephone and the other occurrences in the house, but I began to think that perhaps that was possible. On some days the telephone would not ring at all except for the "unknown" calls, yet several family members and friends would tell us upon reaching us on another day that they had tried to call many times. The calls would go through, they all said, ring several times, and then the line would go dead as though they had been disconnected. We were also unable to call out on our line during those periods. It was impossible to get a dial tone, as though the phone line had been disengaged.

Although Ted took the new telephone back to the store and explained the problems we were having, the retailer's inspection revealed nothing wrong. There was no reason for the telephone not to work properly.

Of all the unusual occurrences in our home, the disturbance with the telephone seemed to have the most negative effect on me. Each time it would ring, a knot would tighten in my stomach from the stress. It unnerved me so much that I began to want to leave the house once and for all. For Ted, it seemed no worse of a prank than turning the light or stereo on or off or making his beer erupt in his face. But to me it felt like a real violation of our peace. It was a frequent reminder that something very strange was happening in our home, that we could not control or stop.

19

THE BASEMENT FLOOD

Ted listened quietly as I talked to him late one night about my serious wish to leave the house. I had tried to adjust to the occurrences in our home, and the children seemed happy living there, but I had reached a point where I no longer felt comfortable being alone in the house. I was constantly looking over my shoulder to see if someone was watching me. It was too unsettling, and I did not want to remain in such an atmosphere.

Ted took my concern seriously.

"We could build a house in that new subdivision on the west side," he suggested.

When I told him that perhaps we should, he looked at me for a moment. He had not expected me to want a new house after all the work I had put into our Victorian home. The paranormal activity, however, had made quite an impact on me, and I felt the need to nestle my family in a house with no history whatsoever. Maybe that was the only way we could finally live in peace.

"Are you sure you wouldn't mind living in a new house again?" Ted asked.

"I think I would be scared to move into another old one and go through all of this again," I told him truthfully.

"We had two other old houses and never had any problems with them," he reminded me.

"I'm just so tired of all of this," I said wearily. "I feel like we need a fresh start. A normal life again in a new home."

Ted suggested we use the computer to research available house designs in the event we went ahead with our plan. I followed my husband up to the attic and connected to the Internet. Within a few minutes, we had the building site online and were comparing a few different designs. There was a reproduction Victorian house plan that caught my eye, and Ted told me that could be our new home if I liked it. As he said that, the Internet connection abruptly failed. Although I tried to reconnect, I was not able to do so. It was completely dead. We finally noticed that the phone jack for our modem had been pulled out of its socket and fairly forcefully. It lay some distance from the wall.

"Do you think someone does not want us looking at new house designs?" Ted chuckled.

I pushed the phone jack firmly into the outlet and did not laugh at my husband's attempt at humour. That was just what I did think, and exactly why I wanted to move.

The next morning Ted contacted a real estate agent and told him we were considering listing our home. A few hours later Mark Gerhen arrived at our door with camera in hand. He would be happy to list our house, he told us, because there were presently very few Victorian houses available for sale in our town. Of the few that were listed, none had been restored as beautifully as ours, and he was currently in the process of trying to locate a turn-of-the-century house that still had the look and charm of that era for the Billings family who were moving into the area. Mr. Gerhen explained to us that, although he had taken them through several homes in the past few weeks, including one in our own neighbourhood, not one of the houses had been completely restored. And that, the real estate agent emphasized, was exactly what his client had requested.

As he walked through our home with its ornate iron radiators, claw-footed tub, and pocket doors, he kept nodding his head and smiling. His camera snapped away as he photographed each room for his records.

Ted had installed an antique water pump from 1894 on the countertop in our kitchen, just for show. We had found it at a flea market soon after we moved into the house. On the wall beside the pump was a large antique oak telephone from 1898 that I had purchased at an auction, rewired for use on a modern phone system. When Mr. Gerhen entered the kitchen and walked over to look at the pump, the telephone's brass bells rang out loudly as a phone call came in. He laughed at how much its loud ring had startled him. I too had jumped, as the old telephone was normally left unplugged. Its bell was deafening, and we preferred using the much more convenient cordless phone with caller identification. Yet the cordless phone on the counter beside me had not rung or registered any incoming calls. And when Ted lifted the antique receiver to see who was calling, no one was there.

The last room we entered on the main floor was the new family room, and Mr. Gerhen was really impressed with the addition. He felt that house would suit his client's needs. In fact, he told us,

169

they would probably want to keep the pump and antique telephone as well. Ted smiled at me, knowing I would never want to part with either item, but said nothing.

"I need to see the basement to ensure there are no problems," the agent told us.

"What kind of problems?" Ted asked, leading him down to the cellar.

"It mustn't leak," he said. "The Billings were very firm on that point."

"Well, we do get a bit of moisture around the walls when it's really wet outside, during a heavy rainstorm or when a lot of snow has melted. But it's never been anything that our dehumidifier couldn't handle," Ted told him honestly.

Mr. Gerhen carefully inspected the dry stone cellar and was convinced that it would meet his client's requirements. Ted showed him where the dehumidifier was installed and again stated truthfully that we had never had a problem with any excess water in our basement.

As Ted led the agent through the rest of the house, I became apprehensive at the prospect of selling it. I was no longer certain I wanted to leave the house after all. That sudden indecision surprised me, as there had been no doubt in my mind for some time that we should move. Now, with that possibility looming, I was feeling a renewed attachment to the house. I wanted to finally understand why all the strange activity was occurring; it felt like a mystery that needed to be solved. Also, I felt it would be unfair to allow an unwitting family to purchase it and then leave them with the same predicament.

When Mr. Gerhen presented us with the paperwork required to begin the process of listing and selling our home, I hesitated. I told Ted I needed a bit more time to think about it, and he looked at me in surprise. It had been my idea to sell, after all, and apparently Mr. Gerhen had a buyer waiting eagerly in the wings for a house exactly like ours.

"I just want a few more days to think about it," I told him.

"Well, that's fine," said the agent. "We can sign these another time. But the Billings are coming into town again tomorrow to look at a few more houses I have lined up for them. Could I bring them through for a showing if they're interested, just in case you do decide to sell?"

We both agreed to that, and Mark called Ted shortly after he had returned to his office. He had informed the Billings about the house and they definitely wanted to see it. They had inquired about the basement, and he had been happy to let them know it was dry as a bone and that he thought the house was exactly what they wanted. We scheduled the showing for 2:30 the following afternoon.

That evening I went into the basement to take some chicken out of the large freezer chest we stored downstairs. As I stepped off of the last stair onto the concrete floor, my foot landed in cold, deep water. Pooled at the base of the stairs, it was bubbling up from beneath the floor as though fed by a fast moving stream. I grabbed some old towels and a mop and attempted to clean up the puddle, but the more I mopped, the faster the water seemed to reappear.

I had no idea where the flow of water was originating. Even in early spring, when the weather was rainy and there was a lot of melting snow, we rarely noticed any moisture at all in the basement. But it was then the middle of winter, and everything outside was frozen solid.

I could not clean up the water and finally called for Ted to come down to the basement. When he joined me, he asked what I

171

had spilled. It did not even occur to him that the floor itself was the source of the water.

"I just found it like this," I explained to him, as I wrung out the soaking mop.

"What happened? Did a pipe burst?" Ted asked. He had been downstairs earlier that day with the real estate agent and it had been, in Mr. Gerhen's words, "as dry as a bone."

"No, Ted. It's coming up through the floor," I replied. "Why would it be doing this now?"

We looked at each other and back down at the flooded concrete. We both knew why.

"I told you someone didn't want us to move," Ted sighed.

"You better call the agent and tell him not to bring the Billings over tomorrow," I suggested.

"Let's leave it as it is for now," Ted said. "Maybe it will look better tomorrow."

When we went down to check on the basement the next morning, we found its condition had worsened. Although the water was contained in the area directly below the stairs, the pool had grown deeper.

As Mr. Gerhen had stressed that the Billings were not interested in a house with a leaky basement, I pointed out to Ted that it would be a waste of their time to view it and see this water on the floor. Ted agreed and tried to reach the real estate agent in his office to cancel that afternoon's appointment. When he was not there, Ted asked that he be paged, but we did not hear back from him.

As Mr. Gerhen never confirmed the cancellation of the showing, we decided to leave before the Billings came so they could go through the house in privacy. Ted, the three children, and Piper waited for me outside in the car while I checked all the rooms one final time to make sure our home looked presentable. Everything was spotless and showed very well, but I could not help but sigh when I went down to the basement and looked at its flooded floor.

I took a deep breath and spoke aloud in my most authoritative voice, as if to mischievous children: "Please be good. Just let these people come through the house and see it today, and stop making this mess in the basement. I know you don't want us to leave, but you can't do things like this." I had nothing to lose, and I did not know what else to do.

I felt a bit calmer as I walked back upstairs. I wished we had been able to cancel the appointment before the prospective purchaser saw all that water, but perhaps the flood would not get any worse following my talk to whomever might have been listening. I left the front door unlocked for the real estate agent and his client, and joined my family in the car. As we drove away, I quietly told Ted what I had said in the basement.

"I bet that will be a big help," he chuckled.

After thirty minutes, we drove back to our house to see Mark Gerlien's car still parked in the driveway. We then drove to a nearby park and watched Rosa, Matt, and Kammie play on the toboggan hill for another half an hour. When we again returned to our house, we saw the agent's car just pulling out of our driveway. We had not expected the showing to last that long once the client had seen how much water was in the basement.

The real estate agent had left a note for us on the kitchen table, written on the back of his business card. I felt certain he would have mentioned the flooded basement but instead read: "Thank you for allowing me to show your beautiful home. They really loved it and think it is exactly what they have been looking for. I will call you in a few days. Mark."

I shared the note with Ted, and the two of us hurried downstairs to see the condition of the basement. When we reached the bottom of the stairway, we could only gape, speechless, at the completely dry floor. Not only had the flooding ceased, but there was no sign of dampness on the concrete to indicate where the large puddle had been.

"Okay, this is a little weird," Ted said.

I was so shocked by what I was seeing that I did not acknowledge Ted's concession that there was no logical explanation for this occurrence.

"No wonder Mark didn't mention anything about the flood in his note," I mumbled.

Ted nodded, and we went back upstairs, closing the basement door behind us.

20

"GO TO THE LIGHT. . ."

Mark Gerhen telephoned us later that week to ask if we had decided whether or not to sell our home. The Billings had expressed a strong interest in the property, and they were eager to make an offer if we wished to sell.

Ted and I talked about the proposition long into the night. It had become such a difficult decision for me. We could sell the house, put all the strange and unnerving experiences we had undergone behind us, and have a fresh start in a new home. Yet, I felt somewhat irrational feelings of sadness and guilt at the thought of leaving. I almost felt as if we would be abandoning the spirits, especially those of children, who were so attached to the location and perhaps, somehow, lost. It felt impossible to simply move away from the house without first doing something to help the spirits do the same.

I wanted to put the matter to rest, and to live in an ordinary home. I wanted us to sell our property for practical reasons, such as job relocation or our need for a larger home, and not because we were fleeing from ghosts. And, I needed help in doing that.

When I had first contacted Rhonda from the paranormal society, she had warned me to be careful with whom I discussed our situation. She had seen other people persecuted for similar claims. They had been fired from their jobs or driven from their neighbourhoods. Yet if we had experienced such strange occurrences within our family's home, surely others must have experienced them in other places too. I wanted to know we were not alone in dealing with such events, but felt isolated because so few people were willing to discuss them.

I pondered contacting Rhonda once again. Unfortunately though without actually visiting the site of the haunting, the investigator felt she had already done everything she could through our e-mail correspondence other than offer moral support.

I then thought about calling Beverly and asking her to contact Dennise for us again, but I hesitated to do so. Because she had been the one to initiate our first discussion of paranormal activity and because her sister was a psychic, I had thought we could confide in Beverly and her husband, Ray, without fearing their doubt or ridicule. Yet whenever they visited us, I sensed a slight uneasiness on their part. I understood though that the disturbances in our home were frightening because they were caused by the unknown, and I had not discussed the house with her for some time.

Although Ted was adamant that he did not want a research group conducting ghost-hunting experiments within our house, I felt the need at least to speak directly to a psychic to see if more information could be gleaned. There were many so-called psychics who advertised their services over the Internet, on television, and in the newspapers, but I did not want to waste our time and money talking to just anyone who claimed to have the ability to make contact with the spiritual realm. I began to research who would be most likely to give me the answers I needed.

I finally found Ronald Planter, who seemed very knowledgeable and gifted in his ability to act as a link between the spiritual world and our own. I scheduled a session with him, and although nervous, I was anxious to hear what information, if any, he could give to me. I had not given him any facts regarding our situation, because I wanted to be certain that what he told me was based on his contact with the spirits and not coloured by my own words.

He began our session with a prayer and, perhaps sensing my apprehension, encouraged me to relax. Almost immediately, he began to describe the group of spirits within the home. He said they told him that they had specifically chosen our family to live with them, which explained the strange connection we had all felt upon first viewing the house and our strong determination to move there.

He suddenly seemed uncomfortable and said he was perceiving intense heat. He asked if there had ever been a fire in the house or somewhere on the property. I immediately thought of the smoke alarms that had blared in the middle of so many nights, and I remembered that Rhonda had asked the same question. I told Ronald that, during my research into the house's history, I had not found any written record of a fire.

He said that he sensed very strongly that the spirits were connected to the actual land rather than just the house. He was being

177

shown that there was something very important within the ground, although that seemed to confuse him. Robert was not certain what it was they wanted him to understand. He kept repeating over and over that they were trying to make him understand that something important was in the ground.

When he mentioned that he was being told about something special that had come up from the ground for me, I thought of the rose bush and asked him if it were connected with the spirits as Dennise had said. He said they were smiling and were happy that their gift had delighted me as much as it had, because they wanted me to understand that they loved our family very much and were not there to frighten or harm us in any way.

Ronald explained that they had been upset about the addition that was built onto the back of the house. The high level of spiritual activity within the house, especially during that time period, was to let us know that they did not want the ground in that area disturbed. And, again, he mentioned that he was being shown that it was the ground itself, and not the house in particular, that drew the spirits to that location. They had deliberately chosen our family to live there, because they wanted us to understand the significance of that.

I made notes during our conversation and recorded what I was being told, but I had hoped for more explicit details. I wanted to know the actual names of the spirits so that I could confirm them in old records, if possible. And I especially wanted to know what we could do to stop the haunting. When I asked Ronald if there was a way for us to help these spirits, he explained that he felt they were not there to be assisted. Rather, they thought they were supposed to be of service to our family, to give us knowledge. And they were trying to show him once more that the information was within the ground.

Although Ronald seemed very sincere and I felt he had a strong psychic sense, the session had not given me the clear-cut answers I sought to achieve a peaceful household.

I did not understand what it was the spirits felt we needed to learn about the ground under our home, and I had no idea how to find out under a house that was a solid three stories and had been built a hundred years ago. I realized, though, that any kind of disturbance to the ground brought about increased paranormal activity, even something as simple as digging a hole in the yard to plant a tree. The spirits may have tried to convey the same information to all the previous residents of the house over the years, thereby creating, with few exceptions, the swift changes in the house's ownership. When I recalled how relentless the disturbances had been during and shortly after the construction of our small addition, I could imagine what the first owners must have experienced after an entire house had been built on the land.

Although I wanted my own family to experience a peaceful life once again, I also felt that the spirits needed to know they could go on their way. So, I finally called Beverly again. I explained to her that we were thinking of selling our home but that I first wanted to make sure the spirits were gone for good. I told her I did not want to feel as if I was deserting them by moving away before I had helped them to leave, too. To my relief, she seemed to understand what I was saying and offered to call Dennise and ask her what we should do.

Beverly called me back that very afternoon.

"Dennise said it is actually a pretty simple process, and if she was able to come to your home, this is what she would do herself. Go from room to room, and tell them over and over again that they don't belong in that house anymore. Tell them to look

179

for the bright Light and to go into it, and that will take them to where they belong now," Beverly said.

"Is that all?" I asked.

"She said that's what she would do. You just have to explain firmly to them that they can't stay there any longer, because it isn't where they belong. Tell them they will be happier once they go into the Light. Dennise said they are probably just lost right now, but you can explain to them where they have to go. She said that should really help. Let me know how it goes," Beverly said, before she hung up.

I went up to the attic and turned on the computer. I wanted to see if I could find any additional help on any of the websites I had previously bookmarked during my research on the paranormal. Several sites mentioned something called smudging, which was the act of cleansing your home of all negative energy and entities. I would need some white sage to perform that, but was not sure if I could find that in our little town.

Later that day I took the children shopping and stopped at a store that sold holistic items. I asked for white sage and hoped the man behind the counter would not think my request unusual. When I reached the shelf to which he had directed me, however, I saw it was stocked with several different types and sizes of bundles of loose sage and smudge sticks.

Back home with my purchase, I re-read the directions given on the websites. And when the children were playing with their friends across the street, I prepared to begin smudging our home.

Ted came home from work a few minutes later, before I had lit the sage. I told him what Dennise had said about directing the spirits towards the Light, and I showed him the websites that described the smudging of the house. He agreed with me that anything was worth a try.

We decided first to attempt to direct the spirits into the Light. I carried a large family Bible with me for moral support and tried to remember all the words Beverly had told me to say to the spirits.

"You don't belong here any more," I said out loud into the stillness of the attic.

Ted and I exchanged glances and then laughed nervously. We both felt uncomfortable performing this spiritual cleansing of our home.

"We shouldn't laugh," Ted told me. "Try to be serious."

I nodded my head and spoke again.

"You don't belong in this house any more," I repeated. "I know you think you are helping us and want us to understand something about what is in the ground here but it's time for you to go into the bright Light that you see near you now. You'll be happier there. That's where you belong."

I started to feel emotional. The words flowed much easier, and I could feel tears stinging my eyes. Ted too seemed more serious, but he was still surprised by how intense I had become. I suddenly fully understood the importance of what we were doing. The thought of the spirits of small children feeling lost or trapped in our house, for whatever reason, filled me with such sadness that all I wanted to do was to help them. I wanted to send them on their way as much for their sake as for ours.

I went from room to room, still nervous and holding tightly to the Bible, but repeating the words Beverly had told me to say.

"Go into the Light," I called out firmly to the spirits, feeling as if I were guiding the lost little souls who had really come to matter to me. "That's where you belong now. You'll be happy there. You don't belong in this house any longer, and it's all right to leave here now. I know you wanted to help us and give us some knowledge about something, but we all want you to leave us now and be at peace," I encouraged them.

After speaking aloud throughout the second floor, I went down to the rooms below and repeated the same words there. When we finally arrived in the family room, I said them for the last time. I looked at Ted and smiled, relieved that we were finished.

"Do you think that will do any good?" he asked.

"I hope so," I said.

I then lit the bundle of white sage and blew out the flame so that it gave off a heavy smoke. Following the directions I had found on a website, I said a prayer asking that all the unwelcome negative energy and entities within our home be removed and no more be allowed to enter. Together Ted and I walked all through the house with the smoking sage bundle. I repeated the prayer over and over as the smoke wafted into every nook and cranny. When we were finished with the sage, I extinguished it in the bowl I had filled with sand. Although the smudging process had been fast and simple, I hoped it would help, too.

After Kammie and I had buried those small objects in the backyard, I had felt a false sense of accomplishment. I had really believed that all our ghostly experiences would be brought to a halt by that one action and had been very disappointed and frustrated when they were not. Although the intensity of the incidents had lessened, they had not stopped altogether. Remembering that, I was cautiously optimistic after following Dennise's advice. Although Ronald had felt the spirits remained in the house because they wanted to help us and did not want to leave. But, if Dennise was correct, and the spirits were lost souls who needed our guidance to find their way into the Light, then perhaps the house was finally free of their presence, and they were finally free of the house.

"Go to the Light..."

The tension or heaviness in the atmosphere of our home had made me feel uncomfortable and ill at ease at times, yet it had also made it difficult to think about leaving. Although I tried to express that to Ted, he claimed he had never perceived any feeling in the house. Although he was a very practical person, he too had felt a strong emotional attachment to the house. That had induced us to purchase it despite the impracticality of our decision. Perhaps the spirits had sensed all along that we were the ones who would finally guide them on their way.

The formerly heavy atmosphere of the house gave way to a comforting sense of peace. I guarded myself against optimistically believing that the spirits were gone and our lives could be normal once again, but there was no mistaking the calmness in our home. I decided we should adopt a "wait and see" attitude before giving any more thought to selling the property.

21

DIGGING FOR THE BACKYARD POOL

After a few months of complete normality within our home, we began to accept that the haunting was finally over. With that realization came the decision not to sell our house just then, even though the guilt associated with moving was no longer a factor. With summer coming, and our coastal cottage being too far away for us to use it much, we decided to install a backyard pool. The children were very excited about it and could hardly wait for the digging to begin.

When they arrived home from school one day, about a week before their summer holiday began, a lot of the work had been already completed. A large and very deep hole had been dug in the middle of the yard. I had only been home for a few minutes after the work had begun and had left Ted to supervise the process. I was as surprised as the children when I got back and saw some of the items that were sticking out of the pile of soil on our lawn. Kammie was especially keen to investigate what had been unearthed.

The first thing she picked up out of the mound was a rusted picture frame. We both eagerly wiped off the layers of mud, hoping to see a photograph, but the picture must have disintegrated long ago. The frame was almost empty, and only remnants of the photo remained along the edges of the glass.

The next thing she found was a gorgeous piece of handmade lace in nearly perfect condition. It appeared to have come loose from a collar or cuff, perhaps from a dress, and looked exactly like the samples from the early to mid-1800s displayed at the local museum.

As she dug through the pile of discarded earth, it soon became obvious that the dirt actually contained mostly ash. This area of our backyard apparently had been the site of a large fire. Most articles were burned beyond recognition, but Kammie found a small pile of school notebooks as she continued to search. They too had been burned but remained legible enough for us to make out the beautiful penmanship in subjects such as botany and arithmetic. When I read the word *botany* on the cover of the book, a slight tingle went up my spine as I recalled the amazing gifts of rapidly growing trees and bushes and beautiful blooms that had been presented to us in the past.

The last article Kammie found was a well-preserved brown glass bottle, similar in shape to a present-day beer bottle, but obviously an antique from many years ago. As she picked it up a large piece of ash also lifted from the pile. A small gust of wind lifted the fragment of ash and flipped it over. There, securely attached, was a tuft of blonde hair. We both gasped when we saw it, and Kammie grabbed my arm. It scared me as much as it did my daughter, but I struggled to keep my composure.

"Whose hair is that? Is it hers?" Kammie said.

"Whose?" I asked.

"The blonde girl we saw with the old-fashioned clothes. I think that's her hair," she said.

"Honey, these things were buried really deeply. I have no idea how long they were there. Maybe it's fur from an animal," I tried to reason.

"It's not fur, it's long blonde hair. And there was a fire. Look at all the ashes. Maybe it killed her. Maybe it killed her whole family," she whispered to me, as though the idea was too terrible to say aloud.

I thought of the children's spirits we had seen over the years: the little boy who ran down the stairs; the angels who waved to Rosa; the young girl who stared at Ted as he slept and who also poked the feather in the ink-well; the sad boy Matt saw by his bed. All of those spirits had blonde hair, as did the woman Beverly had seen by our tree.

I looked again at the antique bottle and remembered how Ted's beer had erupted whenever he tried to drink it, but no other adult's had been affected. Had the father of that family drank too much beer and in a drunkened state caused a fire?

Ronald had said he had a very strong sense of intense heat from the property, and Rhonda had also asked if there had ever been a fire in the house. As the memory of the persistent smoke alarms flooded back to me, the pieces felt like they were starting to fit together.

We found no other items in the ground that day, although we sifted extensively through the soil to see what more could be learned. We even had the construction of the pool halted until we could be certain there was nothing else of importance buried beneath the lawn.

Exhaustive research failed to show any record of a family living on the property prior to the first registered sale and certainly no official indication that anyone ever perished in a fire or any other way. There was no written trace of them at all. According to available documents, the land was owned by the government until 1865, and, if squatters resided there, no permanent record of their existence was ever made.

Those souls, however, obviously had been there and wanted to make their presence known. It was apparently important to them that we knew they had existed, and perhaps also how they had died. They may have wanted to be sure that the tragedy of a fire, conceivably caused by a father's drinking, never happened to another family on that property again.

The conclusion drawn by both Kammie and I when we unearthed those items that afternoon seemed to put all the events we had experienced to rest. The mystery remained as to what the important message was located on page five of the newspapers that had materialized. The appearance of the large nail in our bedroom may have been meant as a warning that our wedding portrait would need better support or it would fall off the wall. Perhaps the appearance of the newspapers and the significance of the message on page five were also intended as a warning, and the true significance would only be revealed in time.

Although the spirits had appeared to leave when I followed Dennise's advice and directed them to the Light, the process had seemed incomplete. We may have helped them to get where they needed to go, but, until that afternoon, we had not understood what they had been trying to tell us or why they were there in the first place.

When we had decided that there was nothing more of import to be found in the pile of earth regarding the property's former occupants, Kammie and I dug a hole beside the "angel bush," as we had come to call the special rose bush in our garden. We gently placed the bottle, lace, hair tuft, picture frame, and school books back into the earth. We said a prayer for them to all rest in peace now and assured them they would never be forgotten. Finally a very real and lasting calm settled upon our home.

We may not have learned their names, but we knew that they had lived there, and possibly even how they had died there, a very long time ago. Perhaps that was all they had needed and wanted us to know. Perhaps that was all they had ever wanted anyone to know who had moved into, and then very quickly out of, that house, decade after decade throughout the century.